The Rise of the Tribulation President

The Beginning of the End

The Black Books Of Moses
Its Secrets And Last Prophecies

Mutti Lewis

The Prophetic Visions and
Dreams of Mutti Lewis
His First Supernatural Encounter

Volume 1 - 2nd Edition
Copyright © 2017 by Mutti Lewis.
Gravity Bridge Publishing

All rights reserved. No part of this book may be reproduced or transmitted in any form or by any means, electronic or mechanical, including photocopying, recording, or by any information storage and retrieval system, without permission in writing from the copyright owner.

Scripture quotations marked KJV are from the Holy Bible, King James Version (Authorized Version). First published in 1611. Quoted from the KJV Classic Reference Bible, Copyright © 1983 by The Zondervan Corporation.

ISBN: 978-0-9994746-0-0
ISBN: 978-0-9994746-1-7

Print information available on the last page.

To order additional copies of this book, contact:
203 685-3262

Contents

Chapter 1: Only Time Will Tell 1
Chapter 2: Some Men Are Given Information Some Revelation.. 10
Chapter 3: The Deadly & Wicked Forecast Ahead... Who Will Be Affected... 17
Chapter 4: The Beginning of The End 25
Chapter 5: The Reason For These Books 31
Chapter 6: I Heard the Voice of The Most High Call Me by My Name 36
Chapter 7: My Supernatural - Encounter "Who Would Believe!!".. 39
Chapter 8: Mother and I Rejoice With Tears of Gratitude 53
Chapter 9: The Closing of The American Dream & The Beacon of Freedom 59
Chapter 10: A Word To The Wise 63
Chapter 11: The Prediction of the Tribulation President Comes True 68
Chapter 12: A Very Serious Conversation with Lando Kerr.. 78
Chapter 13: My Third Vision—September 11 Black Rain Falling from the Sky... 91
Chapter 14: My First Vision & The Strange Visitation.. 96
Chapter 15: It's Not about Religion, But the Relationship with God 104
Chapter 16: I Was Shown Nebuchadnezzar's Dream in a Vision.. 113
Chapter 17: Americans Will Vote with Their Hearts &Not Their Conscience 128
Chapter 18: Is Vice President Mike Pence The Mystery Man In The Puzzle? 130

Chapter 19: The Private Thoughts of The Forefathers of America 136
Chapter 20: America The Mother–Hen of The World & The End of The NRA 140
Chapter 21: Trading Morality for Power and Greed 143
Chapter 22: The Time of Jacob's Trouble Is upon Us! .. 145
Chapter 23: The Chosen Ones: Will Abraham's Seed Matter In The End? 152
Chapter 24: My Dream of The Writing on the Walls of Heaven 158
Chapter 25: The Door Way To Hell 161
Chapter 26: Israel in Great Danger!! Like Nothing We've Seen Before 167
Chapter 27: The Church Painted in Black 172
Chapter 28: The Luke-warmness of God's People 179
Chapter 29: The President Will Be Torn Between The Sabbath & The Sunday Law 184
Chapter 30: And What Will Become of The Sunday Law 189
Chapter 31: The Vision- I Heard an Angel Sing 198
Chapter 32: The Beginning of Sorrow Is Upon Us and the Media Will Help to Decide It 203
Chapter 33: The Great Mysterious Check-Mark of Doom 209
Chapter 34: What We Don't Understand For the Sake of the Elect and the Intent of the Heart 212
Chapter 35: Don't Ever Give Up The Fight 217
Chapter 36: We Cannot Serve God Out of Fear 220
Chapter 37: Will Christ Be The Last Alternative 228

===

DREAMS & VISIONS
THE SECRET BEHIND THE SECRETS
WILL THERE BE ANOTHER GREAT DISAPPOINTMENT?

This is the secret of the Mystery: "If You Love ME, Keep My Commandment, "He said. He never said if you Fear Me"
"The Future is now ... Tomorrow is an idea that may never manifest itself."
The Lord God of The Most High ... Yeshua The Christ ... Who told us time and time again, as it is written, "I AM The Way, The Truth, and The Life ... No man Cometh unto The Father but Through ME."
There is no way around this or above this ... Only those who are faithful unto the END shall be saved.
This is the secret of the Mystery behind the Mystery ...
"If you love Me, keep my commandment."

Acknowledgments

Glory be to The Lord God of The Most High: The Ancient of Days for such inspiration from The Holy Spirit, ever guiding my steps on this illuminous path, that is called the journey of life. The many years of preparation and constant forgiveness of my shortcomings is more than my tongue can tell. With great humility of heart I give thanks for your loving mercies and love towards me always. The visions and dreams are not mine but Thine, because it is You who have sent me, unworthy though I may be… perfectly flawed, but with a willing heart to do thy work. Only time will tell if the dreams and visions I believe you have given me are from you or only a figment of my imagination.

The revelation and inspiration is not my own but from He who reveals Himself unto me. If it is not so, then burn these books, but if it is so I pray that all will come to know Thee before it is eternally too late……..

Special thanks to my wife, Dorr, whose heart of gold has helped to fuel this passion so I was able to write and still keep a roof over our heads. To my children—Rich, Brina, Tash, and Tiff, and also Reece— who often walked softly so I could write these inspirations.

To my dear mother, Mama Lulu, who has been my spiritual guide ever since I could creep and who has always taught the way of the Lord God of The Most High. Her devotion on Friday evening to commemorate the Sabbath and her ever loving hands of chastisement, with wisdom and love, have helped make me who I am. To my dearly beloved Papa Dudley Lewis, who has moved on and is now awaiting the final call of the trumpet of the Most High, I pray we all will be there. To Daddy Barnes (My ex-wife Louise's Dad) and beloved brother Shaw, Bro. Ambersely and Bro. Logan (Bongo Lloyd), these are men of renown. To my dearly beloved brothers, David and Toney Lewis, who have inspired me over the years to become all that I could be—David especially, sharpening and broadening my mental capacity to reach for greater heights. To my sister, Faith (Felly & Veronica) and brother, Ron. To Mouse (Mickey), Brian, Oliver, and Neville, cousin Cyrus Lowe, Mother Mavis, my brother Washington, Raymond, Lando, Howard & Gerald, Dock- Courtney, Charlie, Josh, Sam, Ken, Brick, Malcolm Ashley, Stevie – Dread, my brethren Nigel - Legend & Bowie, Uncle Keith, Gussie ,Farmer-Roots and to all those who have helped me along this illuminous path, my greatest gratitude to all.

Very special thanks to Kay Lawrence, author of "Thoughts from My Heart," for the many blessings and prayers and words of encouragement and for making it possible for this book to get published. Marcie Rodney (who helped with typesetting), and to Rich & Brina for proofreading. And special thanks to my editor, Joanne Willard.

Dedication

Dedicated to The Ones I was sent to—"The house of The Minority," the Children of Israel scattered all over the world. You know yourselves. Also, to whosoever will may come.......

The Author

Mutti Lewis has been on this illuminous path almost all of his life, and has had numerous encounters with The Lord, who has chosen to talk to him from a very tender age. He will tell you of his walks with Him (The Lord God of The Most High), which began around the age of seven.

Mutti was born in the 1960s, the fifth child of his mother, with seven brothers and one little sister. He was born at a time when everything was changing, in a decade of rapid change, with physical and spiritual revolution worldwide during his youth, though few were aware that it was the beginning of the very end of time. It was not until he was taken away in the Spirit and told by The Most High God Himself, "IT IS YOU," that Mutti realized that his purpose on earth might be different from what he thought.

Mutti Lewis believes that no man on Earth should be revered and that you should put your trust in no man, but rather learn to trust The Lord God of The Most High to put your trust only in Him, because He is God, and God Alone. Mutti was blessed with a special mother, who helps guide him along the way. He was also blessed with a prophetic gift that has often given him glimpses of the future and what is to come.

He was surprised one morning in his youth when he got out of bed and found that a gray hair had grown overnight from his right eyebrow, hanging all the way down to his nose. He ran to his mom, frightened by this strange phenomenon, and asked her what it was and what it could possibly mean. His mom answered "I have no definite answer as to what it really is, but don't be dismayed. Time will tell." He didn't want to pluck the hair from his brow, and had no clue where it went.

Mutti has never considered himself a prophet, but rather a humble servant of The Most High God, believing that he was sent for this specific moment in time. He is unpretentious and never hides who he is. He tells the world that he is perfectly flawed and had always thought that prophetic journeys like his were for righteous men and women. With humility of heart, he carries the candle of faith, ever trusting The Lord God of The Most High, who called him by his name as a young boy growing up in the hills of Glendevon—a bird sanctuary, as he recalled it, a forest full of wild birds and the lonely faces of poverty in the ghetto paradise that was his beautiful home. He has experienced his share of the struggle firsthand, which many times has left him on his knees.

He considers himself one of the privileged ones to have met the Lord at an early age, as he often walked in the woods near his home to get away from the struggle of poverty in the ghetto. The woods was the only place he could find peace, listening to the melody of the birds singing songs of praise to The Lord. One day, The Lord spoke to him in the woods, and he would go back as often as he could to hear Him speak. His best friends were his two dogs, Dotty and Lion, who were always by his side whenever he would visit the birch tree in the middle of the woods, where he would become one with The Lord, amidst his daily struggle, as one of the keepers of the flame, though he is perfectly flawed, and believes that he is undeserving of such mystical encounters and Spiritual privileges from A Holy God, whose Spirit does not always dwell with men.

Take the time to find out who Mutti Lewis is. He believes that wisdom only comes from God and that common sense is the epiphany of such a special gift. He was one of his mother's most stubborn children but always had a humble spirit, and when his mother spanked him, he would cry for hours. One day his mother told him that if he ever used that kind of stubbornness for The Lord, he would do great things. This was his greatest object lesson in life, and he often speaks of how those very words stuck in the attic of his mind all these years, and helped to put in place the spiritual blueprint for him to become who he is today—a path that has led him through much pain and sorrow, often finding himself in the valley of the shadow of death. He is humbled that you have taken time out of your busy life to lend him your ears, to see if what he was told or made privy to was meant for you or your loved ones. His salutation to all is always, "Blessed love." He prays and hopes we all may find the essential truth even a day before it's too late.

For Speaking & Booking Engagement & Personal Comment......
Contact Agent- Gravity Bridge Agency
gravitybridgebookingagency@gmail.com
blackbooksofmoses@gmail.com ....

Agency - Phone
203-685-3262

"This book of prophecy, miracles, prophetic dreams and visions with Predictions, will change many lives, maybe even yours, Who Knows?"

It's a chronicle of 4 books of which "The Rise of The Tribulation President" is the hallmark of an epic journey of where He was privy to things that most men on earth only dream of...and read about in the Old Testament. With men like Abraham Isaac and Jacob, Joseph and Moses just to name a few of the patriarchs of old..His story and encounters are modern day old testament, when everything in today's society is packaged in a bundle of organized religion snips, to continue the same deception of control ……………..

Chapter 1
Only Time Will Tell
Introduction to the Chronicles

It has often crossed my mind that perhaps some of us have been asked to create space for more light bearers to make heaven manifest itself on earth. But only to find that an entire civilization can get uprooted because of one man's deranged philosophy, and the sad thing is that men with great intellectual capacity are willing to sit back and allow this to happen. When we think that the globalists around the world that are in power today have our interest at heart it makes us the perfect candidates for a rude awakening. As these last moments in time keep winding down, you will realize that most of us will not be able to see it, much less to try and change it. The secret behind the secret and the truth of the matter is that this time there's nothing we can do as humans to change what is to come, and is now hovering over our heads. The reason is that we are living in a time, when men are lovers of themselves more than any other time before in the history of the world. A time of information overload, intention to cause more confusion, when the heart of man is getting colder each day. Realizing that the grass is growing while the horse is starving, and we allowed it to get higher and higher, as we buried ourselves in our own sad and demoralizing demise. Thinking that creating more chaos to achieve their goals will allow them to create more laws upon the countless laws already in place ,thinking it will help to eliminate the status-quo of man's sin-sick souls, or stop the hemorrhaging of a society that is on the brink of no return. As we create more laws to undo the ones before, we will find ourselves trapped deeper in our own deception, as we barricade ourselves in a deadly plot, creating the monster that they themselves will never be able to control. To make America great again is to come together as one and, make The Lord God of The Most High the beacon of this great nation, giving him his rightful place in our hearts; which would ignite the power of love in our lives and our lights shine in love and harmony so that the rest of the world could see it and get jealous and want to be a part of such greatness. But sad to say this can never happen... total destruction will be the only solution for peace on earth, and for mankind to love again. Instead we will continue to lock ourselves into a deeper bind by our own laws which will surely suffocate us from within.

As we struggle to get out , we become weaker and weaker until the final days go by with only a privileged few reaping the benefit of the masses. You will realize that man is not able to live with themselves without hating and killing each other for no apparent reason other than greed and jealousy. I will ask you a daunting question. One must digest in solitude before answering this very important and timely question.

Does the leaf rot the very day it falls from the tree and hits the ground? What do you think? It's a question that all should take a little time out to digest in solitude, because you are about to face a very gray and bloodcurdling reality, that you won't be able to wrap your mind around.

My next question is for the ones to come, those who will lead this world to the brink of no return and are in the most danger, which are our very children. Did you know there's a bull's eye on the backs of their heads that marks them for death? The truth of the matter is that the more naïve we are, the more vulnerable we all become, but where we stand in the final countdown, is going to be totally up to you and I. It's our children that are the primary targets in this diaspora, even though you can't see it. What we refuse to understand is that, it takes months upon months after the leaf falls to the ground before it rots. Still, it eventually disintegrates in front of our very eyes, and we don't even notice it. Just as none of us can stop the rain from falling or the baby from crying when it's hungry or hurting, in that same mist of the morning, you and I will not be able to stop the flood gates of the great deception from bursting through the levy of a sleeping giant, a society that has been robbed of its sense of reality.

It's the future of our children and their soul salvation that should matter more than anything else in life, but that is no longer the case. This generation is different from all that have come before. The generation of entitlement, who believe that you owe them, the one that most of us as parents are scared to speak to, and because of this haven't told them the grimy truth about life's unkind reality. Instead we sell them a lie that has held them hostage, even though they can't see it. We have given them a false sense of security, camouflage in a bubble of a reality that will come back to haunt them when they least expect it, and eventually destroy many of them that could have escaped such parental atrocity that could have been avoided, if told the truth, from the beginning and given boundaries, and a morality code to live by. Though social media have already captured them and have them like zombies, little lamb to the slaughter still we must fight back.

To love them is not going to be an easy task, but they are our children and we cannot give up on them. If you ever learn to love them for the people they are, and they find a way to love you in return, it will be the greatest joy, but sad to say it will only be short lived. The time has come when they are going to hate you, even when you're trying your best to accommodate them. Only a few will embrace your affection. If something you value gets lost in the rubble of life, do you keep looking until you find it, or do you usually give up after a couple of minutes of searching? We take so much for granted, but it's usually only when we lose it that we really appreciate what we had. This is where we are in America today, at the point of no return where so much will be taken for granted until everything slips away into the abyss of no return.

My next question is, if you have a child that you love dearly, and one day while you are in the park playing with her, you run to search for her little ball she threw into the bushes. You search for a while hoping the squirrel didn't mistake it for a chestnut, they usually hide away for the winter time, as the autumn leaves fall on the ground making everything looking beautiful yet the same. But then you finally find it, eager to see her frown change to a smile, and to become her hero for the day. But when you turn around, she is not where you left her just moments ago. You find yourself gazing in bewilderment, not wanting to believe the obvious, as your fears get bolder.

You look around and realize she is nowhere to be found, as if gone with the wind. What is the first thing that comes to your mind? I know this is going to be difficult for many, worse if you have lost a child to abduction. It doesn't matter whether the child is your own offspring, or a younger sibling, or maybe the child of a friend that left her in your care. The first thing that might come to mind is that someone is playing a wicked game on you, hoping it will be over soon, but as you search and search looking in every obvious corner you realize that it is real. Again, what would you do? Would you drop everything and start chasing around searching for her while crying your heart out? Some of you would start calling the police for help. Would you stand there until help arrives or go looking for her yourself, calling out her name until it echoes back to you, hoping that you'll hear her little voice on the wings of the wind? No one really knows what they would do in a situation like this. In the confusion, some might go running through the park, searching the nearby bushes on their own, even before calling for help, hoping this nightmare will go away. Some might start looking for a suspicious stranger. Everyone you see might be a suspect.

Sad to say ,but this is where we are heading as a country, as one of the greatest societies on the face of the earth. If you have ever been in a life threatening situation, then you know there is no immediately apparent right or wrong answer. All we do as humans is react instinctively to save ourselves if our own life is in danger. If it's your beloved child, a parental instinct can take over and cause more bad than good. Sometimes people die in the process of protecting the ones they love, are you willing to make the ultimate sacrifice to save them from themselves before they're pulled under the murky waters of deception, that are portrayed to be the beautiful sea shore in a California sunset. Today a life threatening situation is hovering over our heads. America, once the poster child for the world, is now like that leaf that has fallen to the ground but has not yet completely decomposed. Similarly, sometimes when the Lord God of heaven and earth gives dreams and visions to the messengers He has chosen to do his work, they will not be realized immediately, but rest assured that if it's God's will, they will come to fruition.

I must open your eyes to some of the things that you can see but will not be able to see, also the things that you will hear but still will not be able to hear, if The Lord God of The Most High does not lead you to it. Sad as it may sound it is real, making preparation for all that is to come that many of us will refuse to believe until it might be too late. Look at the great control man has over man. He has taken a piece of paper that has no value, marked it up and put some dead heroes' faces and numbers on it ,called it money and given power to it. We as human then turn around and worship it;

and would kill our very loved ones for it. Throwing whoever needed to be thrown under the bus to get our share ,even if it cost most of us our very soul. Now what is to come is even more dangerous, and man is getting ready to sell their very children , or children giving up their very mothers and fathers to be tortured for a piece of the great deception, that will be put in front of everyman free and bond to make their own decision. This one carries no prisoners or fence to climb on. No purgatory to water your weary soul of which only the rich would be able to cross over. It is the moment of reckoning that every man who will never come excepts a few who have kept their lamps burning, having extra oil to take them through the greatest darkness that lies ahead. Much, much greater than the dark ages when over two hundred and fifty million souls lost their lives , behind a wicked and sadistic ideology. Man-made tradition that he gives credence to, those who get the chance to hold the handle of such power wield it with much authority. Suppressing the weak as the strong gets stronger. Then it comes down to conscience versus religion another man made theology that will take president over the truth if you let it in the great tribulation that lies ahead. It's going to be the dark sadistic black-hole of the human mind, who chose to pay homage to the prince of darkness; versus the truth, and how it plays out in good against evil, darkness against light.

Does the leaf rot the very day it falls from the tree and hits the ground? What do you think? It's a question that all should take a little time out to digest in solitude, because you are about to face a very gray and bloodcurdling reality that you won't be able to wrap your mind around.

Did you know there's a bull's eye on the backs of our children that marks them for death? The more naïve we are, the more vulnerable we all become , but it's going to be totally up to you where you stand in the final countdown. It's our children that are the primary targets in this diaspora, even though you can't see it. It takes months upon months after the leaf falls to the ground before it rots. Still, it eventually disintegrates in front of our very eyes, and we don't even notice it. Just as none of us can stop the rain from falling or the baby from crying when it's hungry or hurting, in that same mist of the morning, you and I will not be able to stop the flood gates of deception from bursting through the levy of a sleeping giant, a society that has been robbed of its sense of reality.

It's the future of our children that should matter more than anything else in life, but that is no longer the case. This generation is different from all that have come before. To love them is not going to be an easy task, but they are our children. If you ever learn to love them for the people they are, and they find a way to love you in return, it will be the greatest joy, but sad to say it will only be short lived. The time has come when they are going to hate you, even when you're trying your best to accommodate them. Only a few will embrace your affection.

My question is ,if something you value gets lost in the rubble of life, do you keep looking for it until you find it, or do you usually give up after a couple of minutes searching for it? We take so much for granted, but it's usually only when we lose what we have, that we really appreciate what we had. This is where we are in America today, at the point of no return where so much will be taken for granted until everything slips away into the abyss of no return. My next question is, if you have a child that you love dearly, and one day while you are in the park playing with her, you run to search for the ball she threw into the bushes. You finally find it, eager to see her frown change to a smile, and to become her hero for the day. But when you turn around, she is not where you left her just moments ago. You find yourself gazing in bewilderment, not wanting to believe the obvious. You look around and realize she is nowhere to be found, as if gone with the wind. What is the first thing that comes to your mind? I know this is going to be difficult for many, worse if you have lost a child to abduction. It doesn't matter whether the child is your own offspring, or a younger sibling, or maybe the child of a friend that left her in your care. The first thing that might come to mind is that someone is playing a wicked game on you. Again, what would you do? Would you drop everything and start chasing around searching for her while crying your heart out? Or would you take out your phone and start calling the police for help? Would you stand there until help arrives or go looking for her yourself, calling out her name until it echoes back to you, hoping that you'll hear her little voice on the wind? No one really knows what they would do in a situation like this. In the confusion, some might go running through the park, searching the nearby bushes on their own, even before calling for help, hoping this nightmare will go away. Some might start looking for a suspicious stranger. Everyone you see might be a suspect.

This is where we are heading as a country, as one of the greatest societies on the face of the earth. If you have ever been in a life threatening situation, then you know there is no immediately apparent right or wrong answer. All we do as humans is react instinctively to what is in front of us, with the intention save ourselves if our own life is in danger. If it's your beloved child, a parental instinct can take over and cause more bad than good. Sometimes people die in the process of trying to protect the ones they love. Today a life threatening situation is hovering over our heads. Truth of the matter is that America, once the poster child of freedom for the world, is now like that leaf that has fallen to the ground, but has not yet completely decomposed. Similarly, sometimes when the Lord God of heaven and earth gives dreams and visions to the messengers He has chosen to do his work, they will not be realized immediately, but rest assured that whatever assignment or omen that is given to them if it's God's will, they will come to fruition, if not time will tell.

Chapter 2
Some Men Are Given Information Some Revelation
(Introduction to the Chronicles Continues......)

Let me let you into a little secret that many of you, would rather not hear but are dying to know. The truth or what lies in the darkest and most serious moment of earth's history , the secret is the tribulation president is here. It's been a long time coming and some of us have often hoped and prayed that the reality that is in front of us is not real. So many of us are blinded by feel-good religion; hitched to the prosperity bandwagon of the great deception.

My question is what's going to happen when things start appearing in the sky that is not of human origin? Are you going to run and hide when it all starts to happen ? are you going to wish that you had taken heed while you had the chance?

Yashua came in poverty and they rejected Him. Just like many will reject Him again, embracing a false messiah that will come before His great and mighty return, also choosing prosperity over His wonderful and sacrificial love. But who can phantom the mystery of God? In February of 2016 I posted on social media after speaking of it from the summer of 2015 that Trump will be the president and I was laughed at many a times. Here below is a little example of what I have posted on social media, my Facebook page to be exact, and I cut it and pasted it for you to see it in the raw, unfiltered and un- edited and this was long before he became the presumptive nominee. I have spoken of Russia and China and then the pope of Rome of which it will happen in sequence just as how it was given to me. Look at the date and time, and go back to my site and look at the post in its entirety and you'll understand it a little better. If it didn't go the exact way I was shown it I would have put my pen down and walked away from these chronicles that I was appointed to write, because I would be leaning to my own understanding, God forbid. It was never about me but The One who has sent me.

THIS WAS THE PREMONITION............ I posted on social Media on February of 2016

https://www.facebook.com/mutti.lewis/posts/10207187044046999?match=cHJlc2lkZW50IG9iYW1hLG11dHRpIGxld2lzLHByZXNpZGVud-CxvYmFtYSxsZXdpcyxtdXR0aQ%3D%3D

Mutti Lewis

February 29, 2016

IN MY BOOK ....."The Black Book of Moses , Its Secrets & Last Prophecies" You will see the PREDICTIONS of what I have been privy to..... TRUMP will be the next president of the united states of America whether or not you and I like it.....Hillary Clinton will give him a good fight but she will not make it.....Reason is: The stage has been SET for the FINAL COUNT-DOWN of Earth's history, with president Obama ..preparing the way for a president Trump....with the passing of "The MARTIAL - LAW & same sex (marriage) setting the stage for the return of The Messiah Jesus Christ .....as He said ,and I quote "Just like in the days of Noah so shall it be in the end " which is in the last days before His return .....Everything that is happening NOW!! Has already taken place. In the Antediluvian World.....The next 4-5 years from now, will be some of the worst in the History of the world don't take my word for it you will SEE ......president Trump will give the power to the first Jesuit pope ....in the history of the Vatican.... these are the most dangerous men on earth, who assassinate presidents and kings, alike to get their way, these are men who have ignited the flames of more WARS than you could ever imagine...HISTORY & TIME has told all the un-told STORIES .....It is no mistake that pope Francis, is one of the most popular among evangelical, Christians and their leaders ......What president Obama has done....with these laws that he had sign into law , are no mistakes , he was compelled to do it. (no one loves him more than I do , I voted for him twice) and is still inspired by him...one of our greatest presidents, but just like how , Jesus Christ came to earth to die for the sins of men ...and he had to be betrayed....for the prophesy to be fulfilled and by choice Judas played the role......what is to be must be. The stage is set you will have a president Trump on your hand ....whose ego is bigger than himself....who will go up against the other great powers of the world, (because no one else will be able to do it, despite the political pundits who have no clue of what is about to happen) ...which is Russia and China, and for peace sake the Pope will intervene ,and set the stage for the Anti-Christ .....you will see how it all plays out..... I depicted precisely what The Lord has shown me ..in visions and dreams....... I will show you things that are going to blow your minds.....IT'S A MUST READ..... The most important thing , is when "NOTHING MATTERS ANYMORE" where will you and I stand?

Mutti Lewis.....

Also A YouTube Video **Entitled ....THE TRIBULATION PRESIDENT DONALD TRUMP.........**By Mutti Lewis . (The Black Books of Moses)

This video I finally got posted on social media on the 6th of November just days before the election , just to put it out to the world before the election. After so many attempt to get the book out but kept running into stone walls one after the other, by my publisher, knowing that it's not flesh and blood we fight against but principalities in high and low places.

I was able to get a copy of the narrative on GUM-ROAD as an E-Book.

This was just for proof because of the political forecast it contains; Understanding humankind, how unforgiving we can become if I had missed the deadline of the election.

This was when Donald Trump himself had no clue that he would win when it was mathematically impossible for him to win ,when all the national polls had him trailing behind Hillary Clinton in double digit.

You will realize that I have written this narrative long before it was published with Clinton having a 4 point lead on him down to the pole. As you will realize that the number 4 is a prophetic number much more powerful than you'll ever believe. This very premonition of the points was given to me by The One who have sent me yes! The One who speak and reveal things to me. While I was in Jamaica that summer putting the final touches on these chronicles. Snips of the content that is written in this book you will find on You-Tube and also an e-book that was published on Gum-road .

If it was done after the actuality then it would have lost its credibility as a prophetic premonition.

I will reveal something very mysterious to you and you might not believe ,because even I find it hard to fathom that The Lord God would bring me into His glory, a mortal, feeble, sinful man. But let me give you a little snip of what you will see as you read these chronicles

John the Revelator saw the New Jerusalem coming out of heaven ……for some reason The Lord God chose to take me into heaven and showed it to me, undeserving me? . Yes!! I was taken there and what I saw still baffles my mind. It took me years to understand most of it and I'm still trying to understand it all ,but it's impossible.

As TIME goes on and He open the windows of heaven for me to see little glimpses of tomorrow I realize that it's all a mystery within a mystery and all I am is a humble servant of The Most High God and how more than privileged I am that He uses someone like me. Someone who if I was The Lord God, would never think of.

That's how unworthy I am ,but grateful for His wonderful love and mercy towards me. I realized a lot of things over the years, as I walk in humility with The Lord God . My question to you is this; Did you know that God's holy angels sing the songs of mortal men? I heard one of Gods holy angels sings, it's the greatest voice mortal ears could ever heard. Now I understood why Lucifer walked around with such pride, the fact that he was created with the greatest voice of all of God's creation. But he allowed it to get to his head and got thrown out of heaven, having the freedom of choice to choose. How great is The God of heaven and earth to give all of His created beings the freedom to choose. Today you will realize that you and I are no different from the powerful beings of heaven ,that were created perfect and human beings were created just a little lower than them, but have one thing in common which is the ability to choose wrong or right, darkness or the light. It will be up to you to decide what you will do with this information, dreams and visions I was given to pass on to you . it will be up to you to believe or not to believe, at least I have told you; Now you choose.

I received my first vision over 25 years ago and heard the voice of The Creator of heaven and earth speak to me almost 40 years ago. Its only now He tells me to reveal to you the things that He had been showing me or made me privy to. It was confusing at first but now I know that The Lord God cannot make mistakes and it was for this very moment in TIME that He had prepared me for, to come to you as a humble servant though you might not receive it but I pray that you will understand it for what it is . Don't take my word for it, you decide.

Isn't it amazing how We often illusionize the evidence living the moment in denial and hoping that it will all pass tomorrow to the illusion that we want it to be or wish it really is. Today I must tell you the truth you wish is not true, but it is real.

Some have been given information, but only a few are given revelations. It's by their fruits you shall know them. This is where many will be deceived, believing the news media and pundit over the word of The Lord God. As it is written in the Holy bible. Depending on others to bring salvation to them instead of finding and proving God for themselves. Look keenly at what I just reveal to you. If you're wise you will never dismiss it. without bias, some men all they have is information , but those that The Lord has chosen, receive revelation.

For the first time in the history of this great nation, the land of the greatest opportunity, you'll see something that transcends the morality of the American people. How could this be possible? you may ask, in a land where freedom of religion and the constitution are revered and transcend the power of any president, but this time it will be different like nothing you've seen before. There was a time in this great country that if you had the heart and mind to plant a seed and the strength and courage to water it and watch it grow, anything was possible. America is known as the land of the free and the home of the brave, idolized by some , hated and envied by many. The rest of the world looks on to see what her next big invention or next move will be and how it will affect the rest of the world.

Many will not believe what I'm here to tell you, but America being the land of the free is a thing of the past. Pretty soon she will lay down her crown as the beacon of hope and liberty in a volatile unstable world, while all the other nations look on in awe and shock. We will all see our democracy give way to a different order, much more powerful than anything you've seen before.

Chapter 3

The Deadly & Wicked Forecast Ahead Who Will Be Affected?

THE DEADLY and dark FORECAST & A LITTLE MORE

I'll give you a little forecast of what lies ahead, and sooner than you think will be up on your door step. The time is almost here that money will be blowing in the streets, and no one will pick it up. It will overflow into the rest of the world, and many will not understand it and will ask, "What on God's earth is going on?" Confusion will reign in the minds of most Americans and people across the world. If you're not careful to let emotion overpower reason, you may be surprised to find that you've helped to give power to what is to come, if it is not already upon us. Things are going to get tricky and problematic, with money blowing in the streets of the big cities like New York City, Los Angeles, London and Paris, you'll see places like Toronto and Tokyo just to name a few and all of the other great cities here in America and around the world. You will witness it for yourself on television or in real time, the wealthy and the homeless, the wise and the careless, walking by it like there's no tomorrow. People will seek to understand what is happening, longing to hear a word of truth, which will be a rare commodity. We're going to wake up one morning in this same quintessential America, the hub of power, and realize that we are under curfew. Seeing police and soldiers standing at our gates and eventually knocking on our doors, you're going to scratch your heads in disbelief wondering and asking when and how all this happened. And there will not be an answer to your question, because it will be irrelevant to the moment you find yourself in, which will be one day too late. People of all color especially the dark and brown people will be targeted, Jews and Muslims and all of Abrahams children (which are of many nations) will be put under subjection. Those who looks odd or different from the status quo.

People will be lifted from their countries by force, extradited by the thousands to come and stand trial in the courts of America—and it will not be for crimes against humanity, but for breaking the laws that will govern the new world order. This president is going to bring his enemies here to stand trial under the camera of the powerful media that runs the world and shapes our opinions subliminally. It will be the theater of a new world, and the people won't be able to get enough of it. This will be the new normal as the media scramble to fetch their bucket of water from this well of the highest bidder to boost their ratings. This will only give more power to the tribulation president, who will need this platform to accomplish exactly what he is here to do. The secret behind the secret is that he himself does not yet know this. I also know that some of you may be smiling to yourself, saying "Sure! This guy [yours truly] has no idea what he's talking about! " But just as how I saw September 11 approximately 4 years before its actuality, of which I did warned as many people as I possibly could, plus friends and family members alike. I promise you that it's going to be sooner rather than later, and when it happens, your jaw will drop in awe the only thing is that even then many of you still will not believe. Remember these words. Sit back and watch the salvation of The Most High God and sees how it all plays out. Why do I mention money so many times? It's because it is the necessary evil and man-made power that has drawn so many people by the millions to America's shores, away from their beautiful islands and different countries around the world. We all came here for different reasons, but for many it was for a piece of the American pie, attaching our carts to the bandwagon of power fueled by the mighty dollar for over four hundred years. Others sought a freedom unknown or unavailable to them in their home lands. Many came to America with the intent of making enough money to return to their homes and start a business or make a better life for themselves and their family, but got stuck here, seduced by her neon lights and beautiful illusions. And who wouldn't be mesmerized? Before you know it, once you've lived the American life for a while, you realize that you're hooked. Stung by the same serpent of illusion. Pretty soon you realize you became a slave to an idea of freedom, on the treadmill of oppression. As the poor ravish the poor and the wealthiest get richer and richer every day. The bills start piling up, and you become a captive to your car note, your credit cards, rent, or mortgage, to your student loan and the many enticements of the American dream. Pretty soon you won't be able to get enough of it. You find yourself controlled by the very gadgets that were supposed to save you precious time, wasting time on trivialities, until your cell phones and social media control your every move instead of the other way around. No matter what you do, something will get you hooked and keep you here. It's a very hypnotic society, where heaven and hell meet you on the same winding roads. Many with good intentions not to get caught up in it will not be able to return home when it all begins, because it will be too late. Once the greatest power on earth that so many have given their lives for and that many more die just trying to get into will be barricaded with walls more mental than physical. Will they be walls of oppression, built out of conjured up manipulative fear? It's going to be all about mind control like never before. As you look around, no matter where in the world you are at this very moment, you'll get the sense that something is different, that there's a strange feeling in the air that you cannot wrap your arms around. We will be re-fed the healthy diet of racism with whip cream on top of it and this time it's going to be more repulsive, abhorrent and bare face like nothing you've seen before. Don't you realize that something strange and inexplicable is hovering over our heads? What it really is, is that our time on earth is nearly over, slowing to a halt in a countdown to the very last moment of the beginning of the end.

What was shown to me in a prophetic vision is like nothing you've ever seen before—the very same statue that was shown to Nebuchadnezzar and Daniel over two thousand years ago in a prophetic vision. The truth of the matter is that what is about to come upon us is going to be sad. What this tribulation president does will not be of his own creation, but will follow the blueprint of the final countdown to the end of the world as we know it. Many, many things are on the table to be implemented under his presidency, things that he himself has no clue or knowledge of or nothing to do with, but will be given the power to implement. It is for this reason he is here. I don't know how long this countdown will last, but I will show you what was shown to me. In this time the American people will give up their freedom, trading it in for a false sense of security that will never be. The question is, how many know that it will never be. We have forgotten so easily that nuclear weapons do not travel at the height of trees, but come from the sky. Manmade walls cannot stop weapons of mass destruction from raining down on us. We have passed the point of no return. Barricading ourselves from the rest of the world will not protect us but will give the man of perdition (who must come) access to steal the very soul of this great nation in front of our very eyes, as we allow creeping compromise to wear the crown of immorality, which will take center stage and be worshipped as the new deity. Whatever America does, the rest of the world emulates, whether good or evil. Did you know that everything we do in life is a test, no matter how simple or far-fetched it may seem? The things that happen in our daily lives are no coincidence; they happen for a specific reason, with the intention of bringing us one day closer or farther away from the truth. Is it by Divine design that we are where we are today, or is it because of the choices we make each day? This is a question that must be answered by each and every one of us, because from this day onward you will find that your very life is changing. Either we are a part of the problems that plague our world today or a part of the solution. There will be no middle ground when nothing really matters anymore. It will be dogs eating dogs without remorse.

It will be the jungle where only the strong survive. No one will be able to stand on the fence of obscurity hiding beneath the cloak of ignorance, because ignorance of the law is no excuse; everyone will have to choose, sooner rather than later. Not even the youngest children will be exempt; everyone will have to account for their own sins. As far as the children are concerned, the light of those under the age of seven (7) should, hypothetically, be reflected in the lives of their parents. But we serve a God full of mercy and love molded in compassion, so no man on earth knows how He will go forward. It was He who said, "Suffer the little children, to come unto me: and forbid them not, for of such is the kingdom of heaven" (Matthew 19:14). Those who are grown and of the age of understanding, given the freedom of choice, will have to make the decision on their own, knowing that the apple never falls too far from the tree.

One of the executive orders issued by President Obama will, by design, take full effect under the tribulation president. This most rigid and consequential order will allow people to be pre-judged even without committing the actual crime, and to be held indefinitely in an internment camp. The place that we humans have brought this once beautiful world to is a place of sorrow, though most don't even know it. Those who chose to be used by the prince of darkness think they are creating a utopian world without God The Most High to worry about. The dogma of a sin-sick mind is now at the point of fulfilling such prophecy. Today, it's not about me. My silly and gullible days of leaning on my own understanding are gone. Yesterday I feared death, but no longer. What I fear most is not completing this assignment that was given to me, to share with you what I have been shown. Today it's about The One who has sent me. I follow The Lord God of The Most High and wherever He leads me, there will I follow. The secret behind the secret is that all of the moments in time that we take for granted are gems for those who have gone before us, as the sting of death has swept them away into the land of no return and placed them on the permanent shores of their eternity. This is the mystery within a mystery that no person on the face of the earth has the answer to. All those who have ended up on the dark side of the moon figuratively speaking, of which Yashua The Christ spoke in the parable of Lazarus, a poor beggar, and the rich man. Both ended up in the place of no return.

The rich man saw Lazarus in the place he wished was his, and then wished he had made the right decision, but it was eternally too late. He would have given everything he ever owned just for a sip of the water that Lazarus had access to, to wet his scorched and blistering tongue. What men on earth do not know is that the key to the kingdom of heaven is hidden in the mystery of the parables. So much we have taken for granted, most especially the love and mercy of God The Ancient of Days who sent His only Begotten Son, Jesus Christ, The Lord God of The Most High. Billions and billions will live to regret doing so. I pray and hope you won't be among those who reject such perfect love. Many who have gone before wish they had the chance that you have today, to reverse their present status in the depth of a cold sad place, the pits of hell. They would gladly live in poverty just to regain access to God's love and mercy, which so many take for granted, and reverse their current reality.

The secret behind the secret is that we fail to realize this is all a test. Every man on earth must go through this evaluation ,it seems so simple but in the end it will be man's greatest surprise, when you see your entire life on a scroll in real time .The movie or screen play of your entire journey will be in front of you playing out your every move from birth to the very moment you say goodbye and breath no longer exist in the body that was given to us to carry our immortal soul. For those who do not know ,but the soul cannot die the devil cannot destroy it, only The Most High God can terminate the soul. For this reason you will understand that everything you do in life. you must be aware that you and I have been tested. Nothing is a coincidence, just like this president is not a coincidence. You, this very moment reading this book is not a coincidence.

You have been tested, and it's very, very important that you understand this, because this moment is about to be played out bigger than any other time in the history of the world. This time it's not Daniel and his two friends who will be the only ones who will decide not to eat from the kings table, you and I will have to make the final decision that will cement our souls for eternity.

This is the defining moment in the history of the world these 7 last years that is ahead of us. I really don't know how it's going to play out but from what I saw in these visions I can only say God help us!!

Lucifer the devil tempts us every moment of our lives intention to steal our soul while The Lord God of The Most High tests our hearts, to see what they're made of, though He knows the beginning to the end as well as the end of the beginning of the end to the very end of the world as we know it. He knows the very last soul that will make it through the pearly gates before the last trumpet sound. No one both in heaven or on the earth knows this. The secret behind the secret is that Lucifer doesn't have a clue how this will end, he knows what he wish it will be ,but doesn't know what it will be. We're at a very, very crucial moment in the history of TIME as the time –clock of The Most High God counts down to the final moment on His prophetic time–table .

It's the second time in the history of the world that we have come to this moment in time, when all the angels of death have been summoned and given the order to stand alert. They are getting ready to come to earth and devour everything that is not of the Father, having the seal of The Most High on their foreheads. The first time was in the antediluvian world when the death angels were summoned to go and sniff out the hundreds of millions and millions of lives that dwelled upon the earth at the time except for 8 (eight) people which was Noah and his family. I know many of us think it's a joke and rather embrace feel-good religion over the essential truth. Sad to say many will regret this moment for the rest of their lives. Remember we have been tested every single moment of our lives. It's going to come down to the moment when The blood of Yashua The Christ will not be able to save you, because that window of opportunity would have been lost/gone forever if you delay and take these few last moment in time for granted. Welcome to the beginning of the end.

Chapter 4
The Beginning of The End….

The BEGINNING of THE END Of THE WORLD is Upon Us

Though the cruelest of jokes may sound innocent, to those who do not have the capacity to understand what has been said, to those who are much keener what we must always look for is the intent behind the joke. It is not the actuality that man will be judge by in the end, but the intent of our hearts. Again, my first question to you is a simple one, so simple that you might laugh at me, but is so important that I will ask you one more time: "Does the leaf rot the very day it falls to the ground?" The secret behind the secret is that this apocalyptic moment that you and I have been hearing about ever since we were kids is finally here. Yes, it's already here! The leaf on the ground has been disintegrating for a long time now. It's just that you cannot see it. Truly, it was not meant to be seen by all. Having been blinded by the neon lights of doom makes it even more impossible to see. This is the reason I was sent to you, given these visions, and dreams, so you can see for yourself and believe if you choose to believe. In no sense can I force you to listen if you don't chose to listen, and I wish I didn't have to tell you, But I am a servant of The One who has sent me, and I promise to deliver His final warning to you even though I'm running behind time.

Sometimes I wish it was good news I have to give to you and that I wasn't the one sent with the bad news like a doomsday prophet, but I'm not the one who decides the moment we're living in or what message I receive. Just like how Noah was not in control of what he was sent to do but did what he was instructed to do and the rest was in the hand of the one who sent him I often shed a tear or two when I see what is about to come upon us, knowing that most of you are unable to see it, just as Christ cried for us when He was here on earth, knowing the cunning evil ways of the enemy, even though it's right before our very eyes we still cannot see it. In a time when everything is changing man is losing grip on reality, intoxicated by pop culture and all its neon lights of doom, as creeping compromise takes the place of reason and plunges us into the abyss of a dim and grave tomorrow.

What do we expect to find at the end of the rainbow? I can see glimpses of what I was shown in visions and dreams by The Lord God of The Most High, as we paddle downstream to the end of the world as we know it. The sad part of it all that we will live to regret is that so many of us don't seem to care or really believe that the time is here. The mountains and valleys that lie in the forecast of tomorrow's apocalyptic moments will creep upon us like a boa constrictor snake while we are asleep, and you will wake up in a semiconscious state of mind and find yourself wrapped up in its powerful death grip, so tight that you will not be able to move. Every time you try to move or resist, the beast will squeeze you tighter and tighter, and then what will it be next? In the middle of the day you're going to wake up and wish that you are dreaming, only to find yourself stuck forever in this grim reality that could be so different if you had taken the moment in time seriously while you still had time. As we draw closer to what is to come, it's going to be unbelievably sad. It is worth repeating that it's going to feel as if you're having a bad dream or a vicious nightmare and want to wake up from it, but you'll realize only when it's too late that this is the grim reality that we have created for ourselves, and now it's ours to keep. Nothing will really matter anymore, and we will have to live with it. What is going to make it even sadder is that praying for this dark cloud of doom that hovers over our heads to go away will not help. So many of us have been praising The Lord God with our lips, while our hearts are far away from Him, that even prayer and fasting will dissipate the cloud. So many of us will end up in the grip of this reptilian beast, that has come to devour us.

For you to understand where I'm coming from and where I intend to go with these chronicles that tell of the visions and dreams that have lodged permanently in the attic of my mind and made imprints on my very soul, understand that the puzzle given to me is a mystery to figure out. I invite you to unravel it with me and determine for yourself whether my interpretations are right or wrong. I am a mere human given this assignment that I have to try and figure out, not ever wanting to lean to my own understanding but only on The Lord God of The Most High. I can never make assumptions about the visions and dreams I am given, in sleep or in real time, but can only convey to you what is made privy to me. I know it's not going to be easy for some people to believe the things I've seen in these dreams and visions, but I can understand that. Not every friend or family member with the advantage of knowing me and the life I have led can believe some of the things I have shared with them, every time these visions occurs I sometimes find it hard to fathom that The Lord would go out of His way to talk to a sinner like me, a man who is perfectly flawed. I have written these books not leaning on my own understanding, but under Divine inspiration, even if sometimes my words carry you to places where you don't want to go. I myself have been to many places I wish I had never gone. My early years coming to America were a mess, fighting my own demons day by day before The Lord God freed me from my own self-destructive ways. As you follow me through these chronicles, I will tell you a little at a time how I got to this point in my life, some of which seem coincidental, some I am not proud to speak of. My question is, was it by Divine design that it has occurred the way it did? I'm in no position to speak ill of any man, and what I speak of is only to uplift mankind. If it's perfection you're looking for in man, I'm not the one. But I must help you to understand a little of my journey, so at least you're not misled.

Snips of His Journey

Mutti Lewis has been on this illuminous path almost all of his life, and has had numerous encounters with The Lord, who has chosen to talk to him from a very tender age. He will tell you of his walks with Him (The Lord God of The Most High), which began around the age of seven. Mutti was born in the 1960s, the fifth child of his mother, with seven brothers and one little sister. He was born at a time when everything was changing, in a decade of rapid change, with physical and spiritual revolution worldwide during his youth, though few were aware that it was the beginning of the very end of time. It was not until he was taken away in the Spirit and told by The Most High God Himself, "IT IS YOU," that Mutti realized that his purpose on earth might be different from what he thought.

Mutti Lewis believes that no man on Earth should be revered and that you should put your trust in no man, but rather learn to trust The Lord God of The Most High to put your trust only in Him, because He is God, and God Alone. Mutti was blessed with a special mother, who helps guide him along the way. He was also blessed with a prophetic gift that has often given him glimpses of the future and what is to come. He was surprised one morning in his youth when he got out of bed and found that a gray hair had grown overnight from his right eyebrow, hanging all the way down to his nose. He ran to his mom, frightened by this strange phenomenon, and asked her what it was and what it could possibly mean. His mom answered "I have no definite answer as to what it really is, but don't be dismayed. Time will tell." He didn't want to pluck the hair from his brow, and had no clue where it went.

Mutti has never considered himself a prophet, but rather a humble servant of The Most High God, believing that he was sent for this specific moment in time. He is unpretentious and never hides who he is. He tells the world that he is perfectly flawed and had always thought that prophetic journeys like his were for righteous men and women. With humility of heart, he carries the candle of faith, ever trusting The Lord God of The Most High, who called him by his name as a young boy growing up in the hills of Glendevon—a bird sanctuary, as he recalled it, a forest full of wild birds and the lonely faces of poverty in the ghetto paradise that was his beautiful home. He has experienced his share of the struggle firsthand, which many times has left him on his knees. He considers himself one of the privileged ones to have met the Lord at an early age, as he often walked in the woods near his home to get away from the struggle of poverty in the ghetto. The woods was the only place he could find peace, listening to the melody of the birds singing songs of praise to The Lord. One day, The Lord spoke to him in the woods, and he would go back as often as he could to hear Him speak. His best friends were his two dogs, Dotty and Lion, who were always by his side whenever he would visit the birch tree in the middle of the woods, where he would become one with The Lord, amidst his daily struggle, as one of the keepers of the flame, though he is perfectly flawed, and believes that he is undeserving of such mystical encounters and Spiritual privileges from A Holy God, whose Spirit does not always dwell with men.

Take the time to find out who Mutti Lewis is. He believes that wisdom only comes from God and that common sense is the epiphany of such a special gift. He was one of his mother's most stubborn children but always had a humble spirit, and when his mother spanked him, he would cry for hours. One day his mother told him that if he ever used that kind of stubbornness for The Lord, he would do great things. This was his greatest object lesson in life, and he often speaks of how those very words stuck in the attic of his mind all these years, and helped to put in place the spiritual blueprint for him to become who he is today—a path that has led him through much pain and sorrow, often finding himself in the valley of the shadow of death. He is humbled that you have taken time out of your busy life to lend him your ears, to see if what he was told or made privy to was meant for you or your loved ones. His salutation to all is always, "Blessed love." He prays and hopes we all may find the essential truth even a day before it's too late. , then it would have been worth every moment and life would not have been in vain. If Christ was not exempt from pain and struggle, mixed with poverty and much sorrow who am I to complain of mine. The truth of the matter is that without such atrocity, I have no clue of who I would become. Most likely somebody proud and boastful, also full of self, prideful and arrogant of which I would have come to despise in the end when it's much too late. My poverty and many setbacks in life has become my badge of honor, and who else but The Lord God of The Most High could have done this for me when my dreams and passion was to become all that I could be, with the gift of music given to me, intention was to conquer the world with music, but was that my reason on earth? Only time will tell.

Chapter 5

The Reason For These Books
"I Have Never Been Spoken To By An Angel…But Directly By The Lord God Himself."

THE REASON FOR THIS BOOK

Some may find it odd but it is real. This book might be one of the most timely piece of literature you might get the chance to read in these deceptive times , when the world has changed into something that pretty soon you will not recognize. In front of your very eyes you'll be seeing things that you wish were illusions, but will realize that they are real and will only get worse as time gets more advanced and the knowledge of man increases overnight. In a time when there is more religion than any other time in the history of the world yet man becomes less spiritual, replacing the old time religion with feel good and prosperity religion as we drift further and further away from the truth. To understand what moment in time were in you must understand history plus religion to understand the politics of the day. If you have no clue of the past you'll never know where you're going or what to expect when you see history started to repeat itself. Man is always looking for a savior in human , yes someone to tell them what to do instead of seeking the way of The Lord God. Some man take it up on themselves knowing how venerable humankind are , will without a doubt lead them off the edge of the cliff to their doom like lamb to the slaughter.

All of this will be done in the name of religion, power and greed.

It's amazing how the most intelligent of humans will give other humans the power to control them. The ones who desire such positions in the world are mostly men and women of ego and self-elevation. Is it done in the interest of the people or is it for other reasons?

I do not have the answer for all of the above but I will show you what was shown to me in visions and dreams given to me by The Lord God Himself. It's amazing how The Lord choses to communicate His messages to me, truth of the matter is that I have never been spoken to by an angel, In all the visions I have received, but it's the VOICE of The Lord God of The Most High who always speaks to me. I found it very odd and spiritually amazing which put a very significant stamp on what I have been told or made privy to, still it will be up to you to decide whatever you chose to believe. Come with me and let me show you some of the secrets behind the secrets of the world and what is now upon us………..

When I was told by The Spirit of The Lord God, as He often speak to me, about things to come. He impressed on my mind with deep conviction who this president will be amidst the full house of potential leaders that were lined up for the GOP nomination .

It was Donald Trump that came up as the tribulation president but he doesn't know it as yet. When he realizes it he will become bolder and colder as the prophetic time clock ticks away into eternity. As uphill as things seems for him now, it will get calm. (the moral character of the black man/ the minority race will be tested in this time more than ever in the history of America .

It is this resentment of him by the liberals that will ignite the wrath that will inflame the fire in him and allowing him to use every power of his pen as he will sign executive orders one after the other to get his way. The surprising thing is that he will not lose his base who will empower him with showers of praise as America divides deeper than it has ever been before. Things seem now and his feather been ruffled it will calm down.

But after the calm then comes the storm. He will holds grudges and will not forget all those who come up against him. What we are blinded by is the greatest deception, that is about to come upon us.

This He (The Spirit of The Most High God who often speak) did not tell me in a vision but speak it straight to my mind. It might sound a bit strange but you'll understand it a little better as you follow me through these chronicles of the black books of Moses. It was in 2015 after he announces his candidacy for the presidency, running on the GOP ticket; The Lord reveals it to me. Let me warn you a little about this man who is our president in this moment in time. President Trump is a prophetic president like nothing you've seen before. Just like a Nebuchadnezzar with great aggression, he will carry out his policies .

This president will do the same but from a different order. He will not buckle under pressure from all who come up against him. He will wait them out ,and come back stronger.

He is relentless in finishing a task that he puts his mind to, and will find ways to go around the constitution to get his way. Most of the things he does will not look real; as you will say to yourself it's impossible for him to do it , but don't be fooled even if he gets stopped in his tracks at the initial stage, don't get too comfortable he will come back when you least expect it.

He is going to rain on your parade even when the sun is shining. He will do things that are not presidential, and you're going to scratch your head in awe over and over again. He will do things that no other president has ever done before and get away with it, and you will be asking if this is possible in America. The answer is yes this is the beginning of the end of the world as we know it. This has nothing to do with America , she was just chosen as the poster –child to finish the work of the beginning of the end. Just as how Babylon was the most powerful kingdom on earth in the time when the blueprint of the world was given to Nebuchadnezzar ,the secret behind the secret is that that very blue print that Daniel interpreted is now in the hand of the last and youngest power on earth America. It has been handed to this president Donald Trump who will pass it on to another who will be Mike Pence (the vice president) just as how the baton was passed on to Belshazzar the son of Nebuchadnezzar, and it was in this time the power on earth has shifted to a different kind of power that was prophesied long before isreal was taken into captivity. Even the very name of the deliverer was mentioned a hundred years before he was born. It happened precisely as the prophet Isaiah received it. Calling Cyrus (The king of Persia) by his name.

The Lord God of heaven and earth is a mystery within a mystery, He is unpredictable who He chooses to reveal Himself unto.

President Trump will make his mark as the law and order president but will not finish the race, and you will see why.

The stage is set for Jesus Christ to return to earth, and everything is going according to plan, just as it is written. But first the antichrist must come………..This is where it gets tricky and confusing and only God Himself will be able to help us out of this great and wicked deception.

The sad part of this great deception is that most of you will not be able to see or hear it; just like the many dreams and vision that was privy to me and no one else who was in my company was able to see what The Lord was showing me. Even though there are thousands of preachers and teachers all over the world knows the bible much more than I do or will ever be able to expound, yet I was shown these things Is this a coincidence or is it by Divine design?

Chapter 6

This was where my journey began

I Heard the Voice of The Most High Call Me by My Name

I Was Only 17 Years Old

The inadequacy of man's capacity to comprehend the mystery of The Lord God of The Most High is the mystery within a mystery. Many modern days preachers like to brand themselves with all kinds of title and accolades, but why these big titles if not to elevate themselves? Messengers Patriarchs and prophets are appointed by God himself, chosen from among all that He has called because many are called but only a few are chosen. I have only recently come to realize that the struggle of life's journey was no mistake. The secret behind the secret is that these struggles were put in place for the sharpening of our character and for the development of our will and allegiance to The One who sent us.

Why do men on earth give allegiance to and praise men of power and influence? I really don't know because I will give my praise to no one on earth or in the heavens above but The Most High God and Him only will I serve. I will not bow down to angels because they did not create or send me to come to you, and Gods holy angels do not seek to be worshiped. Again, my allegiance is to only The Lord God of The Most High The Ancient of Days. I also did not come to convert or condemn anyone, because that is the work of The Holy Spirit sent by The Most High. What I share with you now might sound a bit strange—that a kid like me (growing up as a youth) who, like countless millions around the world, knew and experienced firsthand the brutal taste and stench of poverty, racism and social injustice was favored with such a supernatural experience. If you don't mind, let me take you on a little journey that has led me to the foot of the cross and eventually to the mountain of The Most High, not unlike Mount Sinai where Moses went to meet with The Most High God, "I AM THAT I AM." For some strange reason, I too was taken up in a vision to meet with The Lord God of The Most High, which has led me to this spiritual and conscious revolution—a journey that is filled with so many mistakes, and so much sorrow and pain that I questioned every step of the way, but I would not trade the experience for the world. Still, I leave it to you to decide if my missteps were really mistakes or were ordained by The Lord to take me where I had to go to reach where I am today, if I am, in fact, where and what He wants me to be. We shall see...... I know that only time will reveal the outcome of this strange and great encounter. Yes, only time will take me where I must go, confirm my reason for being here on earth, and tell me what I must become in the months and years ahead.

Will The Lord finish the work that He has started in me? In the book of time, for every season there is a reason, and for every reason there is a season. Come with me on my journey, and try to make sense out of what some critic and naysayers may call nonsense. "If it is to be, then it's up to me." At the end of this story you will be the judge, and only you will decide as the spirit moves you.

It all started late one summer afternoon, after the evening cooldown from the ninety degree weather that we were so blessed to often experience under the beautiful blue skies over our home in the rocky hills and allowed us to forget, most of the time, the poverty that shared the mountain with us. I grew up on the edge of the Atlantic Ocean that pitched out into Montego Bay off the western part of the island of Jamaica, once considered a jewel in the Queen's crown. It was after the sun had started its slide down over the western part of the mountain, casting long shadows over the hillside that once witnessed my dreams, a place called Glendevon.

It was here that I spent most of my youth; and it was from these mountains that I learned the heart of God and saw His handiworks all around me. It was also here that I fell in love with nature, the backdrop of God's creation. It was here that I watched the beautiful sunsets and marveled at the way the sun often sits on the edge of the Atlantic, as if to cool herself down in the unruffled ocean that embraced her warmth before saying goodbye to a day gone forever. I often wondered then if The Lord God of The Most High could be proud of me for the way I lived that day, as my two brothers, David and Michael, and I had made a pledge among the three of us not to sin against God. We would usually come home in the evening and talk of our day and whether or not we had made our Father Savior and Friend proud of us for that day. I have never forgotten those days, and I know that, come what may, The Lord God of The Most High will remember us, no matter how far we have fallen, and the truth of the matter is that we have fallen deeper than any other family growing up in our church it seems. Our sins were public sins that gave everyone who knows us the chance to point their fingers and judge us. But the one who looks deep within our hearts might someday remember us as children and redeem us one day and save us from ourselves and bring us all back to the fold before it's eternally too late.

Chapter 7

My Supernatural - Encounter "Who Would Believe!!"

"My Supernatural Encounter"

It was in the fall of 1979 when my mother called me four days before the end of summer holiday to inform me of the grave financial situation we were in. I was finally attending the school of my dreams, Harrison Memorial High School. Not knowing if my parents would ever be able to afford to send me to college, I was determined to make the best use of my high school days and honor the sacrifices made by our parents to send us there. It was a great privilege for my two older brothers, Toney and David, who had never really attended a public school (except for Toney in his younger years) as I and my brothers Ranny and Michael (also older than me) and my younger sister Faithy had. And my little brothers, Brian and Oliver, were privileged to attend the prep school within Harrison Memorial without ever having been enrolled in public school. It was a Christian institution and had long had an outstanding reputation both academically and spiritually, as Adventism was known for maintaining the highest standards all the way up through college and university. As a boy I considered a good high school education much more than mere prestige or status. It was a necessity for someone whose reality was poverty and whose only higher education might be in the university of hard knocks been born in the ghettoes. I remember it as if it were yesterday, when my mother called me that unforgettable evening. It seemed as if she had taken the entire day to summon up the courage to say, "Son! I need to talk to you for a moment," and I responded with great concern because my mother hardly ever talked to me like that. She was always the one in charge, in control of what we ate and what we wore to school and church. She was, indeed, in control of her household. Her eight kids were her little chicks and she kept us close just as a mother hen gathers her chickens under her wings to protect them from predators. My father was the strong overseer (enforcing the laws that mother implemented to govern the family) and the one that put the milk on the table, which my mother found so many ways to turn into every kind of cheese, and butter, and even bread. She was not only a mother to her own children but to every other kid that came along the way. Every now and then one would stay long enough to become a brother or sister.

You know who was in control as soon as you entered our home. The respect that my mother demanded was undeniable. She was certain that if she didn't teach us well, we would go astray and the enemy would sweep us up from under her wings, which he tried to do so many times. But the prayers of a righteous man/person availeth much. The only thing that my mother was not in control of was my thoughts, and that was because I wouldn't let anyone in but God and God Alone. I finished what I was doing and went and sat next to her on the front porch. "What is it Mama?" I asked her, a bit scared that she was going to tell me something that no kid would want to hear from a parent, like they were getting a divorce or one of them had a terrible disease. I was a bit hesitant, but nevertheless eager to hear what she had to say. I realized also that she had not called the rest of the family to this particular meeting as she always did if there was a family crisis. But it was only the two of us. My heart was beating a little faster than usual. My brother Toney, who was the eldest of us all and was not around at the time, was always my biggest concern, but he was safe as far as I knew. The last letter we got from him said he was in good health, though worried for our safety as his little brothers, as usual. Otherwise, he was making the best of his journey. As Mother always said, "We are the captain of our own destiny," and she had taught us well. Toney was incarcerated in Puerto Rico at the time trying to reach America and got caught- out for what he had done trying to get us out of poverty and the ghetto of Glendevon, which many didn't make it out of alive. Getting a visa to go to the United States in those days was not easy as a young man who was trying. He had been gone for over three years, doing time for something I could not understand then, and my heart bled for him. It was the same for all of us because he was our hero, the big brother that I emulated, and many wish they had.

Our life was far from easy, for many reasons that may not have been immediately apparent. We were a very close knit family, and what affected one affected the others. David, my other big brother and one of my childhood mentors, took up the lead role when Toney was away, just coming from a siege of bad experiences, with tribal war finally ended and the dust starting to settle, but I feared for him next, because I knew the temper and temperament of his mind. The seriousness that he possessed was buried in silence and he often wore a sad smile. I prayed daily for The Lord God of The Most High to guide his steps, because he had a great heart and because he was my brother. He had much compassion for the poor and needy, especially little children and the elderly, just like my brother Toney did. There are always things that brothers don't agree upon, but we always shared our deepest thoughts and loved each other dearly.

David was always on the devil's list of targets. We all were, but especially David and Toney. I knew that from the time, when I was a little boy, the day that our house almost burned down due to a mischievous unseen hand. David is and always will be my brother that concerns me most. I had seen him that particular morning before he ran off to town to do some errands, so I knew he was safe. My brother Mickey (Mouse) was around the house somewhere, or maybe sneaking out the back gate to play soccer in the street or make mischief as always. He enjoyed poking people or teasing his friends, and a good laugh was his biggest delight. I knew that he was all right, as were the rest of my siblings, so I couldn't imagine what mother needed to talk to me about so urgently. She finally said, "I have some bad news for you, my son," and my heart started racing like a stallion. I know I hadn't done anything to deserve punishment, at least not to my knowledge, and so I asked again, "What is it, Mama?" with hesitation. Solemnly, in the calmest of voices that still resonates in my mind she said, "Your father and I won't be able to send you back to school this semester, and we don't know how long this will last. There's barely enough money coming in to feed the family." She paused and then continued, "As you know, your brother Toney is not around to help out the family, as he always has, and your father's job has slowed down tremendously, and this year the sugar cane and pudding that I sell in front of the house did not do well, because I didn't have enough start-up money to bake enough pudding." Her words broke my heart. I was a bit taken aback to hear such sad news, and the pain in her voice and eyes made me teary, not only because of the sad news but because I wished I could do something radical to eliminate our struggle and take away her pain and change our situation. I could tell it gave her much pain to deliver such a blow to my young mind , but I was never afraid of disappointment, because I had my share even at a very young age and considered it a way of life. I thought she was going to go on, but when she didn't say anything else I was relieved and didn't dare ask if there was anything else. I learned from an early age, "If something is not broken, do not fix it" because in trying you might make it worse. So if it works, let it continue to do so and give God the glory for the blessing. When she did not say anything else, I was glad that everything was all right with the family and before the impact of her news could supplant my gratitude, I paused for a moment and was just happy for my family's safety and the beautiful day I had just experienced. I knew I had to be strong in such gray and gloomy times, come what may, because Mother always depended on me for courage and sound advice even as a boy then, rather than my older siblings, even as a child. The spirit of God that has always guided my steps moved in me, and I knew I could not give up. "I've come too far to turn back now," I said to myself in deep silence. Yes! That little silent voice that speaks to my heart always, spoke to me even as I was listening to my mother's words, and the first thing He put in my mind was fasting and praying. So this was my test as well as my mother's. I knew there had to be a solution and that I had to trust Him more than ever. I had asked Him when I was much younger to allow me to go to Harrison because I would love to become a preacher some day and to lift up His Righteous and Holy Name in great adoration, because by design the world was, and is, getting more callous, cold and outright disrespectful as people take His Righteous and Holy name in vain. I turned to my mother, whom I loved so dearly, and said, "Mama, let's talk to The Lord about it in fasting and prayer," and without hesitation she said, "Yes, my son! Let's do that."

It was at the end of the summer of 1979, on a Thursday afternoon, when she broker the sad news to me, and so we decided to fast the following day, which was Friday. The things that led up to this event would literally change my life forever, and I would see The Most High God in a different light, and also realize that the patriarchs and prophets of old have really met God one on one in their own different ways, and they all communicated with Him and He with them!!! I know that The Lord speaks to the ones He chooses to speak to, at the time and place that He chooses, and this is my story. I told Mama that everything was going to be all right, and she smiled at me and said, "I know, my son. I know!" We had that special secret bond, though she loves all of her eight children. Did it come from humility of heart, or was it from believing, as she did, in The God of our fathers Abraham, Isaac, and Jacob—in the unchanging God whose love and mercy endure forever, in The One whose love is more powerful than his anger. As she has always told me, "Words are inadequate to describe my Lord and Savior Jesus Christ, The King of Kings and Lord of Lords." She often exalted His righteous and Holy name and I praise God with her always, because I believe every word she said about Him.

I come to love and admire her so much for her faith and belief in "The Great and merciful One" that she introduced me to, and I could not thank her more. It's the greatest thing she could have ever done for me, as I too fell in love with Him and could not help it because I realized that He loved me first and loves me more than I could ever love Him.

As a little boy, I realize that my mother loved Him and would do nothing without consulting Him. "He is The God of our fathers" she told me The Lord God of The Most High that I come to know and often saw my dear mother on her bended knees

praying and sometimes singing a song of praise to, sometimes in tears. Was it tears of joy or was it the pain and struggle she came to know which I could not always understand? . The truth of the matter is I don't really know, because The

Lord would never give us more than we can bear, and He loves the underdogs and the downtrodden and we were considered to be among them.

He is The God I came to know because of my mother, the One that she trusts enough to close her eyes and walk through that danger without fear even if its death threat knocking on our door. Our struggle was no coincidence. It is these hills and valleys that have built my faith and love in Him who is God and God Alone. By demonstrating her abiding faith in God, she brought me to love Him even more, just the same as she has loved Him.

We started fasting the next day, which was the day before the Sabbath. That Friday my heart and my thoughts were with My Lord all day as I sang little songs in my heart and told him of my usual struggles and pains. I asked Him to also lift the burden from my mother's shoulders and make it a little easier on her. I know deep in my heart that He was there with me all along and listened to all my questions. After we ended our fast and welcomed in the Sabbath that evening with family devotions, my heart was at peace with both God and man. My brothers and sisters were there, but had not the slightest inkling of what mother and I had discussed and just fasted over. What was strange was that my younger brothers Brian and Oliver and my older brother Michael were attending the same school at the time, but mother never disturbed their spirits with such sad news.

My brother Brian had always humbled himself and worked a part-time job on campus, cleaning up after school, the only school he had ever attended, and I admired his courage. I reasoned that he and Oliver wouldn't be affected, and I was happy for them. I realized that it was going to come down to my faith in God and that my mother told only me because she knew that I trusted the Lord, though I was perfectly flawed. That Sabbath morning I went to church, and the family of God was beautiful, as always. I was looking around with great anticipation because I believed with all my heart that The Lord God had heard the sincere prayers of my mother and me. That very day, the little singing group that I was part of with brothers like Charlie, Ossy, Audley, and Keith, was selected to sing a song of meditation that beautiful and trying Sabbath morning, and the congregation was blessed with our song of praise to the Most High God. Though the words of man are inadequate to speak of The Great I AM, we sang from our hearts, and everyone was blessed. At the end of the service I was hoping for someone like Brother Powell, a police inspector and one of our elders, to come up to me and tell me that The Lord God of heaven had spoken to him of my needs and that he could help me out. When he didn't approach me, I looked for Brother Lando Kerr, who was the treasurer for the West Jamaica conference at the time, a man with a good heart who had always been one of my mentors, but he didn't said anything to me either. As I shook the preacher's hand at the door, I looked at him for a sign, but he only gave me the same warm "Thank you for coming" that he said to everyone else.

I went home for lunch, walking with my brothers and friends as always, saying in my mind, "Lord no one came." I knew I couldn't be discouraged because the day was still young. "It's only lunch time," I told myself, with a solemn smile. For whatever reason, somehow I knew He would deliver. The fasting mother and I had done was different than what we usually do. This time I told her not to worry because God would take care of us. Rather than simply hoping, as usual, that The Lord would answer our prayers, that Thursday I told her not to worry because I believed with all my heart that The Lord would send someone to me and tell me that it was the Lord that had sent him. I really believed this because He had been talking to me since I was a small child. Ever since I was about seven years old, He had been my best friend, yes my secret friend. Only my two dogs, Dotty and Lion, knew because they would always accompany me to the woods and would hear me talking out loud to The Lord under that Birchwood tree about a quarter of a mile from home. They never questioned me or told me that I was crazy. If it had been a couple of human friends there with me, I'm sure they would have laughed at me in scorn and told everyone that I had lost my mind, not knowing that finite minds cannot understand infinite things unless invited to come. For some reason I have always followed my heart no matter how grave the situation is, and after the dust has settled I realize that all I have done is go where The Spirit of the Most High leads me. Unworthy though I am, He understands me better than anyone in the world, and I learned early to put my trust in Him only and not in any man. From a little boy he has put this in my heart. I have been let down so many times by people I thought were sincere, but I know they are only human and therefore prone to err. I have learned this life lesson well and I refuse to forget, even though I have forgiven. I cannot forget because the Lord God of Heaven told me that I must be wise in knowing Him, and I try not to repeat my sinful mistakes. Today, I trust Him to hear my silent sincere plea, and He knows what I need long before I come to Him. When you have great expectations, you have to learn to walk alone. It's never the actuality that counts but the intent of our hearts. And God tests us to see what we are made of. Though he knows us inside out, still we must be tested and tried in the fire if we are going to be one of his humble servants. In the end everything comes down to freedom of choice, as we are told to "Choose he this day who you will serve." I choose to trust The Most High God, in faith without borders, because He is God and God Alone.

That afternoon as I ate my pudding and drank a cool glass of the lemonade that mother made for Sabbath lunch, and even though the pudding was tasty as always (she makes the best pudding!), my mind was somewhere else. It was preoccupied with wondering who The Lord was going to send to me when I got back to the synagogue. Deep within my heart, I knew He was going to deliver. I didn't know how, but I believed.

We were soon back at church for MV (Missionary Volunteer), which was all about the youths of the church learning how to assist and officiate, and develop leadership skills and qualities that would last for a lifetime. It was always a delight for me to participate. This particular evening we sang again for youth meeting—Charlie, with his guitar, always willing to play for the simplest of men. There was a fiery debate as Donnat Darmon and Raymond Grant, two bible scholars, tried to score points in our youth meeting. The church was divided into sections, with youth leaders dissecting the bible's teachings on whatever topic was under discussion, with my brother David and Ossy, Pafus and Michael Montague flexing their biblical muscles and making the dialogue so much more intriguing. That evening was no different. We sang to close out the Sabbath, and walked down the steps of the church and went and stood under the calabash tree that we all congregated under as Adventist youths until we were ready to go home.

As everyone was going out through the gate of our church, I looked and looked around to see if anyone would come, but no one did. With a heavy unassuming heart and a sad smile, I joined the rest of my brethren as they walked casually through the gate. Joining them, I said to The Lord again, in a small sad voice, "Lord no one came, my Lord. No one came." Though bewilderment wanted to set in, I could not give in to it. I still had the same great expectation, though everything looked gloomy, and I knew that no matter what,

I still could not give up. My heart and soul were in constant communion with my Father and only friend, The Lord God of The Most High, and even though I was laughing and talking with my brethren and brothers, I was praying because, though the dusk was about to give way to the night, I still believed that someone would come. When the sun set, leaving yellow and red clouds on the distant horizon, my faith almost went with it, but for some reason I knew I still had to hold on, come what may. As I watched the sun disappear over the horizon until I could see it no more, my hopes grew dimmer. I wondered what I would say to Mother when I got home. It was then that my mind reflected on the faith of Job and Abraham. And as the trail the sun left in the yellow, red, and orange streaks painting the sky dissipated, I realized what a wonderful and mighty God we serve. Come what may, He is God and God Alone. I came to that conclusion because the sun was my marker and if the day was done, it seemed like all hope would be lost. But Mother and I believed that God would answer our prayers. Knowing her, I figured she would still be praying.

It had been a long summer and we had much to laugh and talk about. As we started our long walk home, I still believed that someone would come to me from The Lord. Pafus, Genna, and Burgs started laughing at some joke I could not wrap my heart or mind around at the time, as Tenny, Montague, and Bruce joined us. We were all strolling down Sun Valley road, talking and laughing as usual, sharing stories of the great summer we'd had, but my heart was still in spiritual turmoil. I knew what I had asked the Lord for, and I believed with all my heart that He heard me. I was still looking for Him to send someone to me, though I knew not who it would be. I don't know how I knew, but I did. That is the power of belief. My friends and brothers had not the slightest inkling of my plight or my constant communion with my heavenly Father.

Just as we reached the other side of the church wall, not far from the gate that we just came through, something strange and mysterious happened that startled me, and I couldn't believe that no one else heard what I had just heard. I heard a voice bigger than life itself call my name out of the heavens of heavens, and I almost dropped everything I was carrying. Somehow I knew that this voice was the mystery within a mystery and much more than man— more than anything I had ever heard in my seventeen years on earth, bigger than any of God's created beings. I recognized it within my soul even though He had never spoken aloud to me like this before. But He had been speaking to my heart since I was that young boy going into the woods to find Him when there was trouble at home, and it was the same voice, so I recognized it. The voice that makes heaven and earth tremble at His command said to me out of the heaven of heavens: "Mutti ... Stop!" Unbelievable! What I heard was more than mortal tongue can tell, and words are inadequate to describe it. "The Lord just called me!" I said to myself—the very voice that calms the angriest of seas and stills the raging storm. I stopped suddenly, wondering how on God's earth all of my friends did not stop in silent reverence of the great and mighty voice. I really thought every one heard it, because that's how loud it was. The voice echoed in the heavens, coming from the direction of the calabash tree above the church. I stopped in Godly fear and looked up into the heavens above the roof of our church, from whence I heard the voice of mystery within a mystery. I stood there in awe and disbelief, trying to get a hold of myself. And as I kept looking up, the voice of many waters said to me, "LOOK DOWN," and I turned my eyes slowly from the heavens, hardly believing that The Lord God of heaven and earth was really talking to me. "Sinful me!!" I whispered to myself, and I did look down, not knowing what to expect.

What I saw in front of me was unbelievable, but even more unbelievable was that I, one sinful, perfectly flawed human boy, not always one with God, was hearing his voice. It was the greatest thing that has ever happened to me in my entire life, even now. And what I saw in in front of me was so personal and uniquely beautiful—a pile of money neatly folded, rolled up in a bundle at my sinful feet that had gone so many places they shouldn't have gone. Yet He never denied me His blessings, now placed right at my feet with perfect love and mercy. The object lesson I learned is that The God we serve is a God of order, full of love, mercy, and compassion. By my heavenly Father's hand, I'd been given the answer to my prayer. It was too surreal to comprehend, even though I believed with all my heart. . But in the actuality, it is so unbelievable different, because I was looking for mortal sinful man like myself, but not The Lord God of The Most High, not in a million years. I couldn't put my arms around it that He really cared that much for me(a little poor boy) that He would come in person and do it Himself, who would believe this?. As I bent my knees and picked up the gift of gifts, given to me from my Father's own hands, I could only cry in the deepest of praise and thanksgiving to The Lord God of The Most High, as my heart bowed in solemn adoration and the deepest gratitude my mortal soul could ever give. Who would believe what The Lord God of The Most High has just done for me? I wanted to jump and rejoice and tell the world, starting with my friends, but He said I should not, and I'll tell you why as we continue. I looked up to the heavens and asked, "Lord, should I tell them My Lord?" and in a small, silent voice he said, "No!" As I continued looking up to the heavens in awe and great adoration, I felt a sense of great joy and peace creep into my heart. I could go to school on Monday morning and not have to beg them, but rather say, "Here is my school fee," even though I had no clue how much it was. As my spirit was overwhelmed with joy and thanksgiving, I realized that I had not had to take a single step backward or forward to pick up my greatest miracle, the gift put there at my feet by my Father's own strong and mighty hand! "For little unrighteous me, who is not even worthy of calling His righteous and Holy Name?" I said to myself. But for some reason He heard our prayers and He saw our tears, mine and my mother's. I know that she trusted The Lord more than anyone I have ever known. How can I ever stop loving and serving Him? When I asked my heavenly Father if I should tell the others, and He said no, I realized something very peculiar and mysterious about that answer. I did not open my mouth when I asked Him, and He did not speak from the heaven of heavens so that I could hear his voice echo over the roof of the church when He answered me. The secret behind the secret is that He spoke his answer straight into my mind, just as He spoke to me in my first vision when I was but a small boy.

This was just the beginning of what was to come. I invite you into my little world of supernatural encounters with my Father, The Lord God of The Most High and the things He has allowed me to see, for whatever reason. I remember as if it were yesterday when I would, as a little boy, go into the woods not far from home and meet with my Lord. Whenever my spirit was troubled and I needed to be at peace with Him, I would go to our little meeting place under the birch tree overlooking the playing field a short distance from our house. This is where I often went to talk to Him and where He spoke to me in the silence of the wind.

Chapter 8

Mother and I Rejoice With Tears of Gratitude. "The Lord God Really Answers Prayer"

Mother and I Rejoice……..

I remember something strange that happened one day on my way back home after I had gone to talk to my friend The Lord God of The Most High, Him in the woods. I was standing on the little hill overlooking the field where we usually played soccer, a little boy of about seven then, preaching to imaginary people. I don't know whether I was dreaming or imagining myself preaching to all these people, thousands and thousands of them, as many as there were blades of grass in the field. I guess it was this experience that prompted me to say I was going to become a preacher someday and bring the word of God to the poor and needy and to unbelievers in many countries around the world. The things we dream of as kids sometimes come to pass, and I know my relationship with The Lord has existed for as long as I can remember. From the youngest age, I would go into the woods and talk to Him When my brother Mikey and I would get into a fight, I would go and talk to Him about it, because I preferred living in peace over fighting each day. It saddened my heart, but I would find a little peace of mind as I talked to Him, and He often talked back to me and gave me the peace that surpasses all understanding. Carrying my bundle of money, I dried my tears and hurried to rejoin the gang. I still couldn't believe what had just happened and that they hadn't heard The Voice of the Most High God just call my name. I would have thought everyone living in Glendevon had heard the Lord God of The Most High call out to me. It was that powerful! He called me by my name. Unbelievable! God's timing was flawless. I asked myself, "Is there anything too hard for my Lord to do? I never gave up believing deep in my heart that He would send someone to help me, and look what He did! He came Himself! To God be the glory for the things he has done.

As I walked swiftly toward my companions, I wished that the moment would never end. I also wished I could tell my friends the good news, but I knew I must obey. As I regrouped, I couldn't wait to reach home and tell Mama of the great news of my encounter with The Lord God of The Most High ... to tell her of the miracle I had just received from my Father and Lord. I was so overwhelmed with joy that I was on the verge of tears. Who could have anticipated this? It was the longest mile I had ever walked from church to my home. When I finally reached home, I ran to my mother and said, "Mama! Mama! The Lord has answered our prayers!" She looked at me a bit strangely, with a little smile on her face, and said, "What happened?" I stuck my hand into my pocket and pulled out the little bundle—the monetary gift made more precious than gold to me because it was given to me by my Father's own hand. I placed it in her hand. When she saw it she said, "Thank you Jesus!! Thank you my Jesus, my Lord and friend. I thank you!" We were both overwhelmed with joy as we both try to hold back the tears of gratitude. She asked me how much it was, and I said "Mama I don't know. I gave it to you just as the Lord gave it to me." When she unfolded the neatly wrapped gift of God, she said, "Oh, my God! It is all here!!" I asked her how much it was, and she said,

"It's seventy dollars, Mutti! Thank you, Jesus!" I said. "God is good, Mama! God is great!" Overwhelmed with joy, I tried not to cry and said to her, "All we need is five dollars more." She asked me again how it happened, and I told her my story. Tears came to her eyes as well as mine because of His wonders and love that endures forever and forever. She said, "The Lord has really answered our prayer." I couldn't wait to tell my brothers and sisters of the great encounter and handiwork of God, and his favors toward us as a family. Though Satan tries to crush us into the ground and dampen our spirit, we know that our Savior lives, and I am a living example of His wonders.

He could have given me all of it and much, much more, but The Lord God gave me $70. Seven is the number of completion (as in the six days of creation plus the one day of rest). He also could have sent his angels to deliver His miracle, but He did it Himself. These are the things that baffled my mind for years. He could have given me the $75 I needed for school, but He wanted us to do our part also, because faith without works is dead. Again, I will emphasize that supernatural encounters like mine (which I will never and could never take for granted) were only experienced by the major prophets and messengers of old, God speaking to them One on one. That was constantly on my mind through my childhood and youth, leaving me wondering what The Lord God of The Most High had in store for me to do? I really don't know, but one thing I do know for sure is that this might be the beginning of a special walk with The Lord. If it comes to nothing then it was never meant to be, but if it does I know for sure that it's nothing of my doing but the will of the One who sent me and revealed Himself to me.

When I was ten years old, I had a dream of Joseph, the much beloved second to last son of Jacob/Israel. Even though I was laughed at by my own brothers, Mickey and David, when I told them about my dream, I couldn't help but laugh along with them when my brother Mickey asked the question, just as written in the holy bible, in the story about Joseph and his brothers: "Who do you think you are now … Joseph? And you think you are going to rule over us? Never!!" I laughed along with David, because our brother Michael was so funny, but I did not see it as a joke. I could not tell myself what to dream, and for this reason I often marvel (as do many who know me) at how life has turned out the very way I dreamed it as a child of ten. Coming to America would change our lives and put it all in perspective, as I saw approximately 14 years after my "Joseph" dream as it all started to unfold. You'll find the dream in one of the chronicles.

What many kids take for granted, the ability to attend a decent school, was what had led me to the feet of Jesus and the throne of God. Going back to school that unforgettable Monday morning put me in a different frame of mind. I wanted to tell the whole world, but I did not want to draw attention to myself even though I told all my close friends from church that were attending the best public high schools in Montego Bay. They were also starting a new school term that Monday, but had no tuition to worry about. (Among the best government high schools in those days were Cornwall College, Mount Alvernia, and Montego Bay High, with Herbert Morrison the newest of them all. I used to think about how lucky my friends and their parents were, not having to figure out how to pay school fees and suddenly I was the luckiest of them all to have had such a mystical, supernatural encounter, that only one in a billion here on earth might have ever experience in a lifetime. For some reason The Lord had smiled on me. Was this a coincidence? Or was it by Divine design? The secret behind the secret is that my life could not have gone any other way. I've sometimes wondered whether I would have experienced such a miraculous event if I hadn't been attending Harrison Memorial High. I really don't know, but because The Lord God of The Most high cannot make mistakes, I refuse to question it. What I know is that I had no choice but to have that school fee for registration in order to return to Harrison that Monday morning. If that had not been the case, perhaps He would have given me another test of faith that my mother and I would have responded to with praise and prayer. I know that I had no one to go to in supplication but to Him, the author and finisher of our faith, just as I know that the cattle on a thousand hills belong to Him. When the days of summer have come and gone, we are one day closer to the moment in time when time will be no more. Of the ones that have passed, all you will have is the memories. It's a pity that no one would ever know the conversations that my Lord and I had as a boy. It was these moments that strengthened my faith even then, its roots run deep in the soil of my birthplace. My faith gave me reason to embrace each day with gratitude for being among the living, yet it saddens me to realize how fragile we all are as humans and how far we have strayed from God that people would scorn and condemn those who are connected to Him, as the Catholic church did in the case of Joan of Arc, a peasant girl living in France in the early 14 century.

Her pious mother instilled in her the teachings of the Catholic church, which was synonymous with Christianity at the time of the Hundred Year war between England and France. At the age of 13, she began hearing messages from the Lord and came to believe that the Lord had chosen her to lead France to victory against England. Though she was unable to read, she told the king of France things that she had no business knowing, things that could only have been revealed to her by The Lord God of The Most High. As a teenager, she led the French troops to victory in many battles before being captured by the Anglo-Burgundian forces. She was tried by the Catholic church for witchcraft and heresy because of her claims of communications from God and was burned at the stake in 1431 at the age of 19. It was around the time of Joan's birth that the idea of reform was beginning to arise and John Huss, burned at the stake in 1415 by the Catholic church prophesied before his death that another would come after him, within a hundred years, "that they will not be able to put out his light." This prophecy was fulfilled in Martin Luther, who arrived on the scene precisely 100 years after Huss prophesied. For centuries the men who judged the children of The Lord God of The Most High have hidden behind the cloak of Christianity, aiding Lucifer in bringing about the greatest deception known to man with the intention of stamping out the candles in the dark that The Lord had put in place for His children. Not understanding that "It's better to light a candle than to stumble in the dark," their intention is for us to stumble so that they can bring to fruition their idea of a golden age.

This was my first encounter with the Lord God of The Most High in which He spoke openly to me to remind me that He will never leave me or forsake me come what may if I stay faithful unto the end amidst the perils and setbacks that come with our journey through life. Because we are all human having an earthly experience it's not always easy to understand the mystery of God, but it's not by chance that we are here. I invite you into my journey with Him, in which He has not only spoken to me from His holy mountain in a vision but also invited me to come up into heaven to see the New Jerusalem, the New World that He went to prepare for us.

Chapter 9

The Closing of The American Dream And The Beacon of Freedom……..

The Closing of the American Dream

If you want to make God laugh, tell Him your plans! How many times we find ourselves leaning to our own understanding, not having the slightest inclination that finite minds cannot comprehend infinite things. So often we create goals, visualizing or writing down on paper all that we are going to be and all the things we will accomplish in a certain time period. Who doesn't think and dream of great things if you're a dreamer like me? Some of those things leave mental footprints in the attic of our minds, though we may have no inkling that they are very different from what The Lord God has in store for our lives. I must say that most, if not all of us who claim to trust the Lord often bank on the future while the moments slip away. It's so easy to get discouraged and disappointed when the things we have planned in our hearts and minds don't go the way we planned? Has this ever happened to you? Or is it something you may be going through now, not knowing that for those who trust The Most High God, every disappointment is always for a greater appointment. We must learn to trust God with all our hearts, just as little children put their trust in their parents. It is this kind of faith that will help to break down the walls of the enemy and put our lives in perspective. We have to learn to trust God and God Alone. We have to learn to trust God and live knowing that we fight not against flesh and blood but against principalities and wickedness and powers of darkness in high places. The devil loves chaos and is the master of such, and he also loves when you lose control and start doubting yourself. This is when he comes in and starts whispering in your ears, because he loves gossiping and thrives on our weaknesses. This is how he deceives billions of God's holy angels who were also blessed with freedom of choice, just like you and me. To feast on our souls is his delight, especially when we have developed unrighteous and ungodly habits that will only lead to our own self-destruction.

The secret behind the secret is that the devil's touch, evidenced in our changing habits, is too light to be felt, and too heavy to be broken. We all fall for this creeping compromise, Satan's greatest deception that is about to become our reality if we are not spiritually alert. Each passing day, hundreds of thousands are losing their souls to the enemy of God. Waking to this struggle between life and death, darkness and light, is of paramount importance. One great mistake we all make as humans is trusting the ones who think that they know, but do not know, the path to the kingdom of God. So many of us have never been to the mountain top of the Most High God, where The infallible Mind smiles at our ignorance. In America, a place where the truth is no longer legal or lawful, as she makes her way down a slippery slope back into the past, searching for an illusion that will never be, creeping compromise is already happening. We don't understand that nothing lasts forever and that there's a time and place for everything under the sun.

Today, we are at the beginning of the end of the world as we know it. Just as all previous great powers of the world fell to an even greater power, so shall it be in the end of time, fulfilling every word issued from the mouth of God. He said, "heaven and earth shall pass but not one jot of His word shall come back void." We have come to the end of jubilee. It is now God's time, and He chooses who He wants to choose. It is The Lord God of The Most High that put kings up and He is the One who takes them down. What we are about to face is all by Divine Design. You don't have to take my word for it. Time will tell all of the unknown stories. The question is, will we wake up before it's too late? As the insignificant one, I come to you. You are not obligated to believe anything you don't want to believe, because we are all blessed with the greatest gift given to man by The Lord God of The Most High which is freedom of choice. You must always seek to find the truth in every intention. It is not the actuality that is important, but the underlying secrets and intent of our hearts. There is a reason behind every closed door, just as there is a reason for each of the four seasons, and it is a fact that a closed door does not always have the ability to stay closed by itself. Seek and ye shall find, and "whosoever trusted in the Lord, happy is he" (Proverbs 16:20).

Only those who gain the power of understanding will be able to benefit from the knowledge that I am about to unveil and reveal to you—understanding that to whom much is given, much is required. I am about to show you the secrets behind every secret that was shown to me by The Lord God of The Most High. Although this may seem inconceivable, all secrets are tangible and within reach of one's capacity. If you allow time and space to mentally erase the formidable error and replace it with this essential truth, it might change your life. Then and only then will you be able to find the secrets of the black books of Moses meaningful and might be able to apply it to your own life, changing it forever, for the sake of your own soul's salvation.

The first secret you need to know and rid yourself of is fear. Fear is not of God, and once you are fearful of the devil you're already been conquered. It's like a dog that only bites the ones in whom it senses fear in. It's the fear of The Lord that is the beginning of wisdom. Trust God and live, come what may, but don't be defeated by fear. What I am about to share with you, you are not obligated to embrace. Everyone is entitled to a point of view. And for this reason I feel compelled to pass this wisdom on to the wise. "Ye that have an ear let them hear," it is said. It's a privilege to know the moment of one's death in advance and to be able to prepare for it.

Chapter 10
A Word To The Wise....

A WORD TO THE WISE YOU CHOOSE

How many get the chance for the eternal luxury of being able to consciously decide which door they will choose to enter through in those last moments in time, when nothing really matters anymore … when forgiveness and mercy come and sit by our bedside and wait for us to choose where we will spend our eternity, knowing that mercy of The Lord God of The Most High endures forever. This is the moment that will no longer be available to us as sinful man. This is my fear for those who have not decided to take advantage of these final moments in time before God's love is withdrawn from the face of the earth forever, and man is left to face the consequences. By facing what is to come without the armor and breastplate of God, it will not be possible to make it out alive. What I am about to tell you may fall on deaf ears for many, but a word to the wise is sufficient. Just as the rest of the world turned a blind eye towards Eastern Europe in the late 1930s with World War II looming, it is the very same invisible omen that barricades our shorelines today. What happened then created one of the earth's worst manmade catastrophes, resulting in incredible social, emotional, physical, and spiritual atrocities in the history of mankind. This time it is a different forecast than has ever been seen before. It is similar to the nature of the greatest revenge that now hangs over us like a cloud of doom. It will be upon us before we know it. You don't have to believe me, as time will tell. I pray it won't be too late for those who refuse to take heed, perhaps suffering from information overload and in a state of confusion, not knowing that this is a part of the great deception of the devil.

His intention is to keep you confused and distracted, that it will be too late for those who refuse to heed the last warning. Never in the history of the world have there been more intellectuals than there are today. Yet there is more ignorance than ever before due to the fact that most people lack wisdom. What I am about to tell you is what it is. It will not sit well with many, but there is no reason to be afraid. This is written to prepare you and help you in this very moment in time.

After reading what your options are, understand that there is a chance to escape the worst and most wicked disaster to befall mankind. This has been prophesied, and now it is revealed. Pause for a moment and look around you. Can't you see that most of us are like cattle? We come and go without the slightest inkling as to what is really happening around us, taking everything for granted, as if to say, "It will all be there tomorrow, so I don't have to do anything about it today." Well, maybe for the first time in our natural born life, we have been wrong. The truth of the matter is that we have all been deceived! Where there is no love and mercy and where there is no forgiveness the Lord God of The Most High cannot dwell. To be human as originally designed is rare in these times. Today we are living among people who are not human. As strange as this may sound, it is sadly true. Today, relatively few men and women in the world have a heart. Do you own one? When was the last time you checked to make sure that it is still alive? You might think that this is funny, but you will see what I'm talking about when the stench of this great tribulation takes center stage and you find that you have no more conscience or feelings for anyone but yourself, as men will be lovers of themselves and will be ready to give up their very mother and father to save their own skin from the authorities that will be the force behind the army of men and women that Satan will use to get his dirty work done. But this must come to pass so that the scriptures can be fulfilled. For your own skin, when the time comes you will deny your very child.

You'll be surprised that you will be ready to give up your own brothers and sisters to be put to the stakes to be burned in exchange for food and shelter when the time comes. You may laugh now, but the drought and famine that are in the forecast are going to be terrible, and only those who have made up their minds to take the mark of the beast will be able to buy and sell. They are going to come and search for you to sell you out to the authorities for a profit, God help us! But don't be dismayed. God promises to take care of us who will be here on earth to go through and witness the persecution of the saints. You must have no fear. No matter what, be faithful unto the end, and be a part of those who will inherit the crown of life the Lord has for us. He will never give you more than what you can bear, so buckle your belt for the wickedest ride of your life, because it won't be easy. In the era of the Ottoman empire after they conquered Constantinople, to conquer the Romans—the greatest power on earth at the time—the Ottoman warriors cut off all food supply into Constantinople, and men became subhuman savages who turned to cannibalism because of the manmade famine that was inflicted upon them. No person knows how he or she will act when faced with true adversity. For the elect's sake the Lord will shorten the time, because the level of wickedness that is going to be upon the land means it's going to be terrible, God help us! If you do not hear man say "By the grace of God they will overcome," then you know that they know not what lies ahead and are not one with God The Father. Reason is we are growing more callous, cold, and heartless every day, rushing toward our own demise. Like so many others, I myself have been guilty of banking on the future while the moment slips away. The present moment creeps upon us and leaves without saying goodbye. It has been over twenty-five years since I received the first vision from the Most High, but I guess I was too preoccupied to understand totally what The Lord was showing me, and for this reason I find myself doing everything contrary to the greatest calling any mortal man on earth could ever receive, to be able to see glimpses of tomorrow, just like the men of old that The Most High God chose to reveal His secrets to. Still, undoubtedly, I know it is these hills and valleys that have helped to clear my path, knowing that God cannot make mistakes, so I guess all that I have been through (and I have been brought to the Valley of the Shadow of Death many times) was for this very moment in time. I pray that it is, and that I'm not falling behind in this mission given to me for His own reason.

I wouldn't want to let the Lord down because of my own shortcomings—stubbornness wrapped up in clumsiness. I have been through too many valleys, where I have learned many life lessons that only these valleys could have taught me. I've been through the fire and am still going through it, and it this will not end until I take my last breath on earth or live to see the coming of The King of kings and Lord of lords, The Only Begotten of The Most High. It is very possible that I might live to see Him return to earth in His greatest glory with His holy angels because of the vision that He has shown me with writing on the walls of heaven. I have also been to the Mountains of understanding, of which I have gained much through life lessons that humble me in this greatest mission of my life, so that I can continue on this illuminous path with humility of heart, to carry out God's appointed duty that is given to me on this journey called life. In one revelation, The Lord God of The Most High, the only Begotten Son of The ANCIENT of DAYS, invited me to come up into His Holy Mountain where I met with Him face to face. Though I am perfectly flawed and unworthy of such an encounter, He still called me to come and see Him personally, a privilege I felt was for righteous men, and knowing that I didn't belong there, I was shocked, puzzled, and overwhelmed with gratitude. Many who know me would concur that it is not what I think, but what He Knows about me that I do not know, and I realize that this is what is the most important. That is what matters most.

Chapter 11
The Prediction of the Tribulation President Comes True

If the election of 2016 had not turned out the way it did it would mean that Jesus Christ is not coming as I have interpreted the prophetic dreams and visions I've been telling people about. It would mean that what I'm seeing is not of God. I would be able to put my pen down and rest my head in peace and you would be able to forget about everything I've written about in the four Black Books of Moses. I've been having these prophetic dreams and visions for many years, but I had no clue how to get the message out into the world until I was taken up into heaven to meet with The Lord God of The Most High concerning the beginning of the end what to look for in order to escape the greatest atrocity that will ever come upon the face of the earth. For some reason, unworthy though I am, I was called to come and see The Great One and was given this assignment to convey to you these few words of wisdom. It's up to you whether or not you believe them. In 2015, I was given the prophecy of a Donald Trump presidency by The Lord God of The Most High, in which Trump was appointed by Divine design as the Nebuchadnezzar of this modern day Babylon, to take the world into the apocalyptic era as the tribulation president—a president unlike any of the 44 presidents that preceded him. He will be the lamblike beast who speaks like a dragon, which is a double-edged sword between him and his vice president, Mike Pence. This president will be swift in action, as I saw in the vision. Events will happen so rapidly that our heads will be spinning, like nothing we've ever experienced before. Spiteful and vengeful, he will hold grudges and will not seek to live in peace with his enemies. His will be the kind of strength that is needed to bring this world that is on the brink of self-destruction to a halt. Once it does, all hell will break loose, as I have seen it in a vision. It will be this president that will take us to the end of the world, that causes the Nebuchadnezzar statue to turn upside-down, and after that all I can say is God help us!

I was invited as a guest by Rass-Imell, a very conscious brother, the humble lion on WDJZ at the time, radio host and general manager of a community radio station in Bridgeport, Connecticut. I told him of the prophecy I had been given that leaves me with great concerns. I also gave the revelation to other brethren, including the man who speaks without apology: I –Messiah of WPKN 89.5 FM. I was compelled to tell many more acquaintances of my premonition, from the very beginning of the 2016 presidential race when the political stage was crowded, and the news pundits thought that Trump was the circus master and failed to take him seriously. They still have no clue as to what lies around the bend, that Donald Trump is a prophetic president, that he is about to take the world into a tail spin, and that the entire earth will be affected by his policies, which he will make boldly and without apology. This is much bigger than the Republican party and the news pundits know, as most of them cannot even see through a glass window, much less into the future. I was shown a glimpse of God's prophetic time clock of what is to come. For reasons known only to Him, The Lord God of the Most High has shown, or made privy to me, snips of the future and glimpses of His prophetic timetable of what lies ahead. The abomination of desolation is upon us, lurking in the dark, hiding in broad daylight, and we are all too mesmerized by the great deception of Satan in the everyday hustle and bustle of life to recognize it, or even suspect what's going on. We are so immersed, by design, in pop culture and Band-Aid religion to see the grave danger that lies ahead, hidden under our very noses. Most newscasters are paid big salaries to regurgitate or reiterate what is given to them. I understand this, as every one of us has a part to play in this great mysterious puzzle that still baffles the most brilliant minds on earth today, which is an integral part of the great deception. The ones who have the power to control our emotions and the way we think and do things are working tirelessly to achieve his agenda. ... I got a glimpse of what is around the bend, and it's not pretty. If God doesn't shorten the time for the sake of the elect, as He has promised, it's going to be much too sad to see what is hanging over our heads and what is to come. I was given the appointment to write these four books, collectively entitled the Black Books of Moses: Secrets and Last Prophecies, and because of this I was submerged in daily devotion to this special spiritual appointment. Consequently, television and social media have become a thing of my past in these days of relentless labor and one-finger typing, as the words of God as given to me flow like a river through my mind, and capture it all has not always been easy.

It is sometimes tedious, I must say, my clumsy typing and imperfect command of grammar slowing down the process immensely. These books were supposed to be in your hands long before the election, but I was bombarded with setbacks as part of the spiritual warfare that we must fight every day as God's children—not against flesh and blood enemies, but against principalities and wickedness in dark and high places. A segment of this book was published in an e-book (which you can find on GUM-ROAD) before the November, 2016 election because of the political forecast it carried. The greatest thing I pray is that when my work is done you may be able to understand it for what it is, and if even one soul who has never met or known The Lord God of The Most High comes to know Him from these writings, then my living on earth will not have been in vain, and if one who has been associated with another religion, especially my Jewish and Muslim brothers, should have a change of heart, I will be happy to have helped them find the essential truth, as I was sent especially to the house of the minorities.

BURN THESE BOOKS

On the night of the election, November 8, I was in deep meditation, writing, when the phone rang. It was a brother of mine, Dr. Dock Courtney, asking me if I was watching the election, and my answer to him was, "No, I haven't watched television in months now." He then said to me, "So you're really confident about your prediction/prophecy." I said, "Yes, I am!" He asked me why I was so confident. I smiled and said, "Because I only write what the Lord has told me to write." I went on to say, "If these visions are not true, as The Lord God of The Most High has given them to me, then you can burn the books." He asked, "Are you really that confident?" I said, "I have only written what I was told, and what I saw in these visions. If what I write about these visions and prophetic dreams is not true, burn these books, because it would have made no sense for me to go on writing. It means nothing to me, because it's not about me but about The One who has sent me." So if it's wrong, if I have leaned on my own understanding, may God forgive me! And it would simply means it's not Him who has sent me. Perhaps Might be it's just an illusion. But if I am right, and you are around to see it come to pass, I pray that it will not be too late for you to see and be at one with The Lord God understanding the essential truth given by The Lord to Abraham as it manifest in his children Isaacs,

Jacob, Moses and all the others who understand it for what it is. Given to His children for a specific reason for a specific people in this very moment in time and whosoever will may come if you believe.

****

Beginning before sunrise on the morning after the election of November 8, 2016 many of the people who heard the premonition that was given to me in 2015 called me up early in the morning just as the day was breaking , some sent me text messages. The first of them was Josh Barnett who woke me up because I had spent some time talking to him of what I was privy to and some of the things that will come in these last days, I also spent all night writing to finish the rest of the chronicles so that you can have them to know what is to come as The Lord God of heaven and earth opens the windows of heaven so that I can see little glimpses of tomorrow. The hardest part always is to understand what I'm seeing, so keep me in your prayers that The Lord will give me the correct interpretations of these glimpses, if it is His will. Because it's not my will but His that will be done. I know that we are living in the time when He will allow some to see, but they still will not be able to see, some will hear but will not be able to hear, reason is that we have tuned out His words from our hearts, trading them in for the illusion and glamour of the moments in time that some of us can never get enough of. I pray that He will give me the true understanding of these visions for the benefit of mankind in this time. I know that his love is much more powerful than His anger, so I trust Him to be true to His words always. I myself have benefited from His mercy. Undeserving though I may be, He has still shown me His love, so I know that He will deliver His children from this last episode of earth's final and most catastrophic events that are to come to fulfill the prophecies, that were written over the centuries by the men and women He has chosen, to give glimpses of tomorrow. As St. John 16 bears witness to The love of The Father (The Ancient of Days) Proving His mercy is more powerful than His anger: "For God so loved the world that He gave His only begotten Son that whosoever believeth in Him shall not perish but have everlasting life." I wish I was sent with good news, but the truth of the matter is that I was not. It is because of the seriousness of the latest visions that have been given to me, with great urgency in this forecast, that I cannot keep silent and must give it to the world and let you decide for yourself, as The Lord has given it to me.

I was shown three visions of writing on the walls of heaven, of which I have given you a few in this book because of its urgency and the fact that Israel might be in imminent danger. Knowing that as soon as tomorrow comes everything is different than yesterday, as the moon gives way to the rising sun to break the dawn, knowing that to find yourself among the living is a blessing by itself, the question is, what will we do with it? You and I have another day to make the right decision, but many did not get the chance to see the sun rise this morning or to hear this essential truth in the raw. This simply means that you and I may be among the ones who will not perish in the end, even if death is on the horizon for our souls. Understand that God's children are not exempt from such spiritual and physical atrocity. Know that in the end, when nothing really matters anymore, your soul will not perish with the unbelievers and naysayers who refuse to acknowledge Christ The Messiah as The Only begotten of The Most High, much less accept Him as their Savior for, as He said: "I Am the Way, the Truth, and the Life. No man cometh unto My Father but through Me." It's been over two thousand years now since He came to earth and made this statement, and most of the people that have hated Him and are still hating Him have never taken the time out to know Him personally—the greatest missed opportunity of a lifetime, which many will live to regret just like the antediluvians in the days of Noah who are waiting for the final judgment. I could speak of hell, because I had a glimpse of such in a dream that was given to me, but I choose not to use scare tactics, because only love, not fear, can save our eternal souls. There's nothing that can compare to His love, the love that conquered the world. Today you and I have the chance to be in the first resurrection if we do not live to tell our story. And if we do, and live to see The Lord God of The Most High break the clouds of heaven in that great getting- up morning, how much greater yet that would be. It wasn't long after the election that I gave a call to my editor, Joanne, and she said, "I can't believe that what you wrote in these chronicles is really what happened." She was the first to read my words outside of my immediate circle of family and close friends (who question much about the visions I have been getting). Joanne had edited the first e-book in a rush, trying to get my message out before the election because of the political forecast. (A prediction isn't a prediction if it's made after events have already proven it to be right!) An avid consumer of political news and opinions, she wanted to know why I was so convinced about my premonition when Hillary Clinton was so far ahead in the polls and apparently headed for a resounding victory. I heard the same thing from Steve, the general manager of WPKN FM radio, when I brought a friend to see him shortly after the election. Always the intellectual, he said, "It's surreal how all the newscasters got it wrong, with every national poll that matters having her as the inevitable winner." What we don't know is that it is The Lord God of Heaven that was, and is in control of this extremely important election that will set the tone for the rest of the world and a very gray tomorrow. "This year, 2017, will see such tremendous changes in the world that it's going to make our head spin" I said to my friend at the end of our conversation. Don't take my word for it. Let's sit back and watch the salvation of The Lord God of the Most High. My reason for saying all of this is that most of the people I have run into are shocked, stunned by something I was privy to months in advance. I was even given the very number of points (four) by which Hillary Clinton would be leading down to the very last hour of the polls. I had no clue what the number meant at the time, because I hadn't watched any television for months.

I was more taken aback by the reaction of a young man by the name of Mark, who invited me to come and give a talk to his little group that meets weekly to discuss end times prophecy, when he saw the political forecast of the Black Books of Moses come true. I have posted on You Tube, and what he said had amazed him was the precision of the detail of the prophecy in predicting a four-point lead. I wonder how much it would have affected the world if I had been able to publish this book a few months before the election or posted it in cyber-space in mid-summer, when The Lord gave the numbers to me. I had been writing for months and just could not bring it to fruition quickly enough. I only had time to put the narrative into visual and audio form on November 1, 2016. I had to overcome many hurdles, hills, and valleys just to get it something in front of the world to solidify the prophecy, which I knew would make or break this very important premonition.

****

I have no choice but to hang my faith on what I was shown, knowing that if the prophecy is wrong, it would release me from my appointed duty given to me by The Lord God of The Most High Himself when, in a vision I had just before flying to London three years ago, he said out of the heavens, "You did not call yourself. I have chosen you." I would never come to you if I had not been sent on this mission. What would it profit me to lie to the world about the word of The Most High. A sinful, fallible man has no business in God's business if not called. Why should I give Lucifer the glory by lying to you? How would it benefit me when my very soul is hanging in the balance? No, I couldn't lie to you. I would rather live in obscurity as a hermit than lie about the Lord God of The Most High, when I am unworthy to even call his name. I call him by His rightful name always, because the enemy of God, Lucifer, is using our children to desecrate His name. He picks our children off as easily as a lion snatches up a gazelle that has strayed from the herd. The Lord God of The Most High already came and conquered, but because we forget so easily, I was sent to remind you that the moment is nearing, and is already here for many who may come to know Him because of what He has shown me. He has taken me in vision into the heavens so that I could come back and let you know not to be deceived by this wicked old serpent they call the devil.

The Lord God has shown me the New Jerusalem that He went to prepare for us, and words are inadequate to describe it. It is this mission I was sent back to Earth to tell you about, in the words in these little books that were given to me to give to you. I pray that you will heed them before it's eternally too late. I was sent back to remind you of what our Savior The Lord God of The Most High Jesus Christ has already done. He put a permanent wedge between you and this devil they call Lucifer, and it is up to us to reclaim it. I will show you what the Lord showed me when I was taken into heaven. I can't tell you how crucial it is for our youth, and for their parents, to understand what I was sent back to tell you with such urgency.

I am the first to admit I've dragged my feet in delivering God's message, and I have already asked forgiveness for it, though I might not deserve it after taking The Lord for granted over the years. I am so unworthy of His love but somehow He still chooses to love me, I can't understand why, but maybe someday I will.

Chapter 12

A Very Serious Conversation with Lando Kerr

Don't Be Deceived & Who Can Decide For The Most High God?

I had a great conversation with one of my boyhood mentors when I visited him in Jamaica in the summer of 2016 when I went there to put the final touches to this manuscript, The *Rise of The Tribulation President…(.Black Books of Moses)*. It was an electrifying day, yet sacred, as my mind reflected on the things and people who have helped make me who I am. We often meet under the same calabash tree where I had argued my point with a preacher who was no different from the Catholic priests back in the days of the dark ages, who sold indulgences in the dark years before Martin Luther, (the great reformer), exposed the fallacy of being able to buy salvation after living a life without consciousness of one's true self, or any real attempt to learn of the Lord God of The Most High, much less to be faithful unto the end. Yet I was ostracized for being a representative from the tribe of Levi, wearing locks upon my head, in the image of the One who has sent me, The Lord God of The Most High. Amazingly it was above the same calabash tree I had heard the voice of The Lord God call me by my name on that faithful Sabbath evening when I was only 17 years old then. That was the day that changed my life forever and made me realize that the God of heaven and earth, creator of the universe, does indeed speak to little poor boys like me, though so many in the world who think they know everything claim that He hasn't spoken to man in hundreds of years. But that day He had called me by my name and change my life forever as He blessed me with my first miracle. It is He who put His hand on my head as a kid and comforted me, and its Him who also knows everything about me. As an earthly father would call his son and speak to him, that's how The Lord God of The Most High had spoken to me, as a Father to a son, though I'm only a humble servant perfectly flawed and without a doubt, unworthy of his love. The day of my visit with Lando was unlike any I had experienced in a very long time because I was bumping into people I hadn't seen in almost 35 years— people like Fernando, a high school classmate, Margret, a beautiful British-born friend that grew up in Jamaica with us, one I had admired dearly in my youth, because she was smart and beautiful, and having a sense of defiantness to her demeanor of which I was attracted to. Margret's sister Carol and her aunts, Betty and ILlah, I saw them all in one day. It reminded me of the good old days as it has taken me back to the days of my yesteryears, when we were all innocent and gullible yet so beautiful, yes! (Memories of our youth often stay with us forever.) I was elated to see them all in good health and Great Spirit despite the struggles of life that we all face on our own mystical journey. I realized that we were all still holding on, which brings joy to my soul. I was hoping to see Olive and their brother David, but I guess just seeing Margret and the rest of her family was joy enough.

Jamaica was indeed the birthplace of my love for people and life, and the spiritual aspect of my being was planted and watered and took root right there in Glen-Devon, where I learned the rudiments of life on an illuminous path in a beautiful yet sad and dreadful world. Though it is full of darkness, still I light my little candle so as not to stumble in the dark, a path I had to find and choose for myself. Was my journey into the unknown by Divine design? It is a journey that has taken me to so many different places, some of which I wish I have never gone to and am reluctant to speak of. It was a conversation with Tatlyn, daughter of the late Brother Ambersely, a man of God whom I dearly loved, that made me realize the importance of where I came from. When I heard Tatlyn sing, "We know we have just begun, and we feel like moving on, but the tide might turn one day but will we be able to stand again?" – words from the song I was privileged to write for my Harrison Memorial High graduating class of 1981 – I knew how blessed I was to have grown up there, among such beautiful people. I also ran into a man by the name of brother Logan (Bongo Lloyd as I know him) who was my neighbor as a boy. He holds great significance in my life as I saw him walking in righteousness even before he found the essential truth. Seeing all of these dear people in one day was a blessing to my soul. These are people with a sense of purpose and sincerity of heart, who have all influenced my life somewhere along the path. I was elated to see them all. Under the cool shades on the east wing of the church, I engaged in a blissful conversation with Lando Kerr, a scholarly mentor of the gospel of Jesus Christ, and Fernando Bloomfield, a school-mate of mine whose mother taught me English in my early years in high school (she was a beautiful lady, indeed, may she rest in peace). I was happy to see that Fernando was still grounded and not enmeshed in the social fabric of Adventism.

It was a vigorous and enjoyable debate. We learned from each other as iron sharpens iron, as though a blind man were in the midst of us, asking questions about the journey of life on this spiritual path to the end of the world as we know it. At the time of our conversation, in which I spoke of the things to come, including the election of Donald Trump as the tribulation president ushering in the New World Order, when political pundits and the polls saw a Trump victory as highly unlikely. His harsh rhetoric and goal of overturning a GOP establishment who thought they were in control of the things to come had him down in the polls, by double digits at the time. But I told Lando that in the end Americans would vote for the first time with their hearts and not their conscience, in fulfillment of Revelations 13. I knew that he would win, despite all the evidence to the contrary, because The Lord God of the Most High had revealed to me in numerous visions that the end of time is on our door steps, with the stern warning "Do not be deceived." Things never before seen in America politics now are the new normal, which will only get worse as it spirals into the abyss of no return. Welcome to the new reality of the beginning of the end. As I explained to Brother Kerr, and to many others from the moment of Donald Trump's announcement of his candidacy for the Republican nomination, all will come to fruition as I have prophesied, as revealed to me by The Holy Spirit of The Most High God, by The One who has sent me. Brother Kerr said to me that it was not possible for this man, Donald Trump, to win the general election come fall, and I asked him why, His reply was, "The gospel is not yet preached in all the world," and that answer scares me deeply, and has caused me much concern. My reply to my dear friend and brother was, "We will all be deceived if we ever believe such a lie of the devil, the father of deception; a conversation among the people God has blessed with the essential truth is devastating." I reminded them of how William Miller misunderstood the prophecy in 1844, in The Great Disappointment, which turned out not to be a disappointment but rather the great appointment that would give birth to the essential truth with the advent message that would prepare the world for today.

It is this very moment in time that The Lord has waited upon with a sad smile to see how many of us will come through. The fact is that the eternal code cannot be broken, but everyone will have to decide for themselves where they will spend eternity. This is the most important question I will ask you to consider as you journey with me in the Black Books of Moses, a question that must never be taken lightly for even a moment, and the question is: will your zip code or postal code be in heaven or will it be in hell? This is the million dollar question for each and every one of us. It will all come down to freedom of choice. My friend and mentor Lando Kerr was ill at the time of the conversation, he could not stand up on his own and have to have someone to bare him up whenever time he wants to walk as if some kind of disease has paralyzed his lower muscles. For some reason this has never dampened his spirit and his conversation was as keen and vigorous as always, shedding light on the essential truth. My heart cry for him, to see him in that state but I couldn't let him know it, because a man like Lando you can never pity because of his optimism for life. He taught us survival skill in our youth Pathfinders club. He was the captain for that ship for many years and hates to see weakness in men, so self-pity even when he is hurting would be catastrophic. At the end of the day when we said our farewell with great admiration I looked at him and said "all will be well my brother" and with the same smile of enthusiasm he said "I know Mutti I know" As he tell me to give his love and regards to my brothers David and Toney who was both incarcerated at the time (trying to overcome the struggle)and as always asked how

Charles was doing. I hugged him and Fernando and shook the blind man's hand, and reminded him that all will be well. It wasn't long I reached back to America I had a premonition that I saw Lando Kerr on the pulpit of Glendevon singing the song of meditation all by himself with no one assisting him. I called my mother and told her that brother Kerr will be well, and just to keep on praying for him until light breaks through. I pray that we will meet again to finish the conversation of the great conclusion.

The Dreams - Big Drops of Rain Falling from the Sky & The Spiritual hoax "Jesus is Coming on Christmas Eve………

The days to come, as the Lord has shown me in vision, will be unbelievable. You will not have enough tears to cry when everything starts happening. In one prophetic dream one of the shortest of all my dreams I saw rain falling out of the heavens like stones falling from the sky. I was standing in the middle of the street, when suddenly without the sky changing into a cloudy and gray sky to prepare us for rain, as the sun was still shining out of nowhere suddenly without a warning, I saw falling from the sky big drops of rain. These drops were as big as ice cubes, as in the plagues that are prophesied to come upon mankind. Why is the Lord God of The Most High showing me these things, if He did not want me to sound the warning? And why would He send me to you if these things that are to come were not almost upon us? My next question is: Why did the Lord God Of The Most High use so many different prophets in the days of old, to prepare the way for his first coming, and also to warn his children when he was about to do something very drastic when His people failed to obey His ways? The answer is that the Lord will never do anything without a warning. Don't you think that He will do the same for us in this time before He return? The secret behind the secret is that we have been deceived with feel-good religion of pop culture otherwise known as prosperity religion, but only if we know what is hovering over our heads, if we know we would all cry-out in unison "God help us!!" hoping he will hear us to make this moment in time pass if it was possible, if we only know. The Muslims claim that Muhammad was the last prophet and that there will never be another.

That was 1,500 years ago, and many things on the face of the earth have changed drastically and without a doubt for the worse. My question is how did we get so deep in the business of The Most High God to decide for Him who The Great I AM must send and who He cannot send? Isn't this a bit absurd and preposterous? The secret behind the secret is that The Most High God is God and God Alone, and no mortal can dictate to Him how He must run His universe. Who do we think we are? Can finite beings comprehend or understand the infinite? The answer is no! He is God and God Alone: "Forever Was, Forever Is, and Forever Will Be." It was 7 of us that were called up to His holy mountain from the tribe of Levi.

The unanswered question that often plagues my soul is nothing you are no man on earth can help me with, but The Father Himself. I have been wondering for years now, who are the other six men that were called, to come up into His holy mountain with me, and where are they now? This is the question that baffles my mind day and night. Everything is going to happen so rapidly it's going to make our heads spin. It's going to be a sad, deadly, and swift journey to the end of the world as we know it. The signs of the time are everywhere, and we are too blind to see them. It's going to be so sad for many who think they have time to play-church to the end of the world; as we know it. What we must never forget is that the Lord God of the Most High cannot make mistakes. The world was blessed 170 years ago with a prophetess, one that many of you might not have heard of before—Ellen G. White who experienced her first vision shortly after the Millerite movement culminated in the Great Disappointment of 1844. The question is why would The

Lord God of The Most High use a woman for such an important mission, in a time when the role of women was being downplayed? This is very, very significant and I will show you (In We all Have Been Deceived) the secret behind the secret of such to show the infallible wisdom of God. For those of you who are unfamiliar with this event, Miller was a Baptist preacher who started a movement based on the prophecies in the book of Daniel. Based on his study of the prophecies, he predicted that Jesus Christ would return to earth in the year 1844. He sounded the alarm and many people came to the fold and prepared themselves for the end. On the appointed day, nothing happened. Jesus Christ never came and the Millerites were sorely disappointed. Many lost their faith, and it was this very event, called the Great Disappointment, that changed the paradigm of Christianity in America and the rest of the world. The secret behind the secret is that Jesus Christ could never come on that day, no matter how diligent and dedicated they were as Christians and biblical scholars.

The Lord God of The Most High said that no man on earth or angel above knows the day of His coming but His Father, The Ancient of Days. But the Millerite movement was much more significant than any would believe, as it was a day on God's prophetic time clock that was to usher in this very moment in time. In vision I have seen Ellen White among the great reformers of the world that were the chosen of God—reformers like John Huss, John Calvin, and Martin Luther. What was even more significant was that Abraham Lincoln the 16th president of The United states of America (and one of the most significant if not the most significant) was among the reformers that were shown to me in this vision. The question is what is it that The Lord God is showing me that I'm yet to understand? You'll be surprise of what was shown to me, its mind boggling to say the least.

For Ellen G White, her work was more significant than anyone would ever believe. The secret behind the secret is that she was the American segment that was put in place by The Lord God Himself to commemorate the reformation started with men like John Huss in the 14th century who prophesy of the one who will come after him ,and Martin Luther came one hundred years to be exact after him. It was Luther's 95 thesis that turned the world upside-down ,breaking down the man-made barriers of Christendom Intention to keep us chained to the dark ages when the catholic church rules the world. Ellen White was sent on earth to commemorate the work of the reformers, all of them Sunday worshippers, was this a coincidence?. It is the intent of our hearts that is of paramount importance to the Lord God of The Most High. It was never the actuality of our deeds. God knows whose intention is to serve him and get carried away into great deception, knowing that we fight not against flesh and blood but against principalities and wickedness in high places. The Lord God of The Most High knows who really loves Him and who is only pretending to love Him. So many of us praise Him with our lips, but our hearts are so far from Him. Can a man fool God? He will raise up men and women from every corner of the earth and every religion and denomination to do His bidding according to His will on His own time clock. The reformers of the 14th century were all of Catholic origin, which was the power on earth at the time, where the church was more powerful than the states. What we are taking for granted today many men and women have given their lives to make this possible. John Huss' prophesy of Martin Luther (one of the greatest reformer, who was the straw that breaks the camel's back) Can a man judge The Most High God? Didn't Christ scold the Jews when he broke the corn on the Sabbath day and eat it?

They claimed that He had broken the Sabbath, when He is God of the Sabbath. As Mark 2:27 stated "The Sabbath was made for man, and not man for the Sabbath" it is through this very gate the reformers will walk and many will scratch their heads unable to comprehend the mystery of The Most High God. It is the relationship with the Lord God that is most important, our hearts He knows exactly what lies within; if it is pure He will find a way to save us from ourselves and keep us out of the vicious jaws of the hungry lion seeking whom he may devour. "Blessed are the pure in heart for they shall see God" – (The Beatitude.)

The Spiritual Hoax – The voice "Jesus is Coming on Christmas Eve?"

In these times when everything is changing for the worst and Satan will be more cunning and deceptive more than ever, only those who are on their guards will overcome. Don't ever believe that salvation was meant to be easy, because it was not meant to be and I will emphasize that only those who are aware of this great evil that hovers over our heads will overcome what is to come. I dreamt that I was at this place an arena it seems with much people sitting on the bleacher stand, or it might be a baseball field I find myself. There were two sets of men on the stand like rival gangs or men with different philosophy or beliefs. I couldn't understand why we were there. All I knew is that we were greeting one another in friendly and Godly fear, with love as brothers and sisters, as I go around shaking everybody hands, and they did receive me with joy and a sense of hope to where we are going. Was I sent there in the midst of these men and women? I really don't know, because some of the dreams just take me to places unknown to me. Some I flew there or taken by The Spirit of God, while some are just regular dreams. It is the spirit of discernment that often makes me be aware of what is shown to me. Sometimes the interpretations takes a little time for me to understand them while some comes with the dream or vision. I never hear an angel speak,(because they have never spoken or allowed to speak when they are sent to come) I only heard one sang, of which words are inadequate to describe, with the limited vocabulary of man. Today I take nothing for granted as He (The Lord God of The Most High) has been speaking to me all along. If I falter I will be held accountable and so I will tell you everything I see that has spiritual connotations to it, and let you decide for yourself as The Holy Spirit will be the One to lead you into all truth and not I. My mission or assignment is to tell you, it will be totally up to you to decide what you chose to believe. All I am is the messenger who has nothing to do with the message.

I can only tell you what is shown to me as The Lord God speak to me. For the first time I heard a voice echo through the wind and I do not know if it is a friend of God giving the warning of a deception to come, I really don't know. You be the judge. As the dream continues I was taken to another place, there were lots of young people mostly white kids I must say, and they were looking up to me to say something, and I did not speak, for whatever the reason that I don't understand, knowing that in dreams and vision everything is for a specific reason. Why was I not permitted to speak at this time, I really don't know. One of them had some kind of pin or needles between his teeth, and I was amazed at what he was trying to accomplish. Just looking at him I felt pins in my throat as well. But what I realized is that people were fellowshipping. It seems as if it was a time of revival in America, people coming out from everywhere. They were all in one accord. I went from there to another and I saw the same thing, men and women gathering outside to hear some preacher preach. It was a festive day it seems as I walked towards the place they congregated. When I reach the place a Caucasian brother was kind enough to get up and gave me his seat, as he was leaving at the time. As I was there I realized that everyone was so nice. This time I was conversing with the people which was mostly whites, and a much older crowd, as the preacher himself was also a white brother. As I sat there listening to what he had to say. Without warning I heard a voice out of nowhere echo through the sky coming from the North, blowing in the wind as it echoes across the fearful, mysterious sky saying "**Jesus Is Coming On Christmas Eve!!!**" and then nothing else comes from the sky.

I looked around to see if I could see the angel who made the announcement. I know that what we all heard bellows through the wind coming out of the sky is more than man, but whose angel would made such an announcement for all to hear, and then I wonder if they hear what I have just heard. None of them were in awe of the voice coming out of the North as loud as a the horn of a freight train up close, with mysticism all around it.. I chuckled to myself, knowing that it's the voice of deception I heard. I really don't know if I was the only one who heard it, but what I know, it does nothing to my heart like when the voice of The Most High speaks directly to me leaving foot prints in the attic of my soul. I knew for sure that this was a spiritual hoax as I smile to myself wondering if anyone else heard it blowing in the wind or was it meant for only me. What Satan is trying to do is to set us up, and I know that he is after my soul with a vengeance. But The Most High is my shield and protector. What Lucifer would love for me to do is to go and announce to the world that Jesus is coming on Christmas Eve. I guess who plan to come or make his appearance is The Antichrist himself.

We must be aware that the devil will try any trick to lead Gods children astray. Don't be deceived as the great disappointment was in 1844 when they all prepared themselves for the coming of the Lord which was the William Miller Prophecy and many souls got discouraged and Gave up the faith, and many have lost their way. Reason is "no man knows the time or day of The Lords return but His Heavenly Father "The Ancient of Days" they were disappointed because they did not totally believe every words of the bible and was leaning to their own understanding. For this reason (those who turn away from the faith) they did not carry enough oil in their lamps. Jesus Christ speak of the 10 virgins, 5 were wise and 5 were foolish. Which one of these categories will you fit into, the foolish ones or the wise ones? The answer is yours to keep. There is always a counterfeit that we must be aware of. Lucifer will do anything to bury what was given to me to give to you, that you'll be amaze to know. Whatever The Lord shows me must line up with His words of the essential truth "If you speak not according to the laws and to the testimony of Jesus Christ is because there is no light in you" Isaiah 8:20

Chapter 13

My Third Vision—September 11 Black Rain Falling from the Sky

"September 11…….. That came to pass"

The Lord has shown me many things, some of which I didn't pay much attention to at the time. These things The Most High gave me accumulated over the years, because I never understood what they meant. But when He showed me what was about to happen to New York City, I knew I had to sound the alarm to warn God's children. I told close friends and colleagues that I knew would not dismiss my words as the ranting of a lunatic, as Noah was scorned and mocked while building the ark. In truth, I warned only those my spirit could be at peace with and those the Spirit would lead me to. It was about twenty years ago when I got this vision, and this one was different from the rest because it was so graphic and haunting, painted in black and white, like a black and white movie that haunts your soul, like the ones you never forget. To this day my dreams come in color, while the visions still come in black and white and shades of grey. It happened in 1997 while I was living in the city of Bridgeport, Connecticut, at 528 Laurel Ave. I went to bed one Friday night after family devotion, and in the middle of the night I had a vision of the events that four years later would change the world forever, putting into place the elements for The New World Order. I was taken away in the spirit by The Lord and was shown something surreal: two huge birds flying through the air side by side. They looked like American bald eagles. As they flew, I could tell they were coming from the north and headed south, because their direction was from Connecticut coming towards New York. They were not flapping their wings, yet they soared through the sky at a moderate speed. From where I was standing in the vision, it seems as if I were witnessing this catastrophe from the vantage point of a high building. As they approached Manhattan something strange came over me, when suddenly the unexpected becomes the reality of the day, like nothing you've seen before.

The birds without warning suddenly started spewing fireballs out of their mouths that exploded like bombs upon the ground. This caught everyone by surprise, and people were running for their lives. It was like hot rain falling from the sky as buildings tumbled down, and people in the street started catching fire. Everyone was in a panic as chaos swept through the city. As the people in the street ran for their lives, they screamed and hid wherever they could. After much damage and ruin, surprisingly one of the eagles did something strange and significant. It took a right turn towards the George Washington Bridge as the other continued, with much destruction, flying over the Hudson River and then south towards New Jersey. You could see the devastation from the fireballs hitting the Manhattan skyline as fires burned in the streets, and dust and rubble from the buildings fell to the ground. It was like a war zone created by two fighter pilots, except they were birds of prey. People stampeded over each other as the panic escalated, and then everybody ran towards Grand Central Station, running down 42nd Street and towards Spanish Harlem, trying to flee the pain and despair. Those who did escape were running and looking back, while scrambling to get out of the city. Everybody was running in one direction it seemed, or was it because of where I was standing? I don't know. But Spanish Harlem, largely ghetto, was the place of refuge. From my vantage point in the vision, all I could see was chaos and great disaster—a disaster as graphic and cold and calculating as could be. It was surreal, and I wondered, "What on God's earth could this mean? Was this the sign of the end of time? Or the real coming of The Lord God of The Most High (Yashua the Christ)? When I awoke from the vision, my heart was pounding, as if I had just run a marathon. I was very much saddened by what I had witnessed. It was then and there that I knew this wasn't just a dream, but another vision.

I realized that this was a warning because of what I felt inside, something that wouldn't let me keep it to myself. Again, this was the third time I had dreamed in black and white with such graphically precise detail and mysterious hints of things to come. At the time I did not have the slightest inkling of the realities that lay ahead in the unknown mystery of the future, or that The Lord was showing me something or preparing me for a specific moment in time, which is now.

The First Revelation

It was this experience that let me understand that these were not mere dreams but visions. They've all found their place in the attic of my mind and are indelible. As one of the prophets of The Most High wrote, "Shall a trumpet be blown in the city and the people are not afraid? Shall there be evil in a city and the Lord had not done it? Surely the Lord God of Heaven and Earth will do nothing but He revealed His secrets unto His servants the prophets" (Amos 3:6-7). The Lord God of Heaven, The Ancient of Days, will do nothing without a warning because He reveals Himself to those He loves.

I told many people about this vision in the year 1997 when I received it. One of my friends, Sandra Russell, who attended Calvary Seventh Day Adventist church at the time, encouraged me to tell the congregation, but I was a bit unsure how they would take it, as I was not a regular attendee. I usually spent the Sabbath in the mountains, in nature with my family, so I was never an insider, and knowing how skeptical the church members could be, I never pursued the idea of telling the entire congregation. Instead, I would tell people that I cared for about how the end of the world as we knew it would come to pass. I never thought the revelation would come true in my time, so when Lorna called from her job on September 11, 2001 and asked me if I was watching what was happening in New York, I casually responded, "Not really. What is it?" She replied, "A plane just hit the World Trade Center." I dropped the rake I had been using for lawn work and ran inside. I turned the television to CNN and watched in total shock. Within less than two minutes as I was there watching, another plane came out of nowhere and flew straight into the second tower. I was in disbelief as the news started airing what was happening below on the ground. My heart sank as soon as I saw the people running in the rubble.

That was when witnessing the catastrophe in real time hit me the hardest. All I could do was sit down on the couch, and say to myself, "Oh my God!! This is exactly what I saw!! Look at the people running out of the city with the dust and rubble all over them, just like I dreamed." My knees shook a bit as I sat down saying, "Oh my God! You showed me this over three and a half years ago, and I didn't tell everyone because I was afraid they wouldn't believe me. But today it happened just as you had shown it to me." I spoke to The Lord God of heaven, with my head down. My spirit in distress as my right hand tugged at my beard as I thought about the eagles in the vision representing angels. The wrath of God seemed to be coming down upon us, not as angels, but as two 747 jets whose destination was set for chaos in NY City. The third jet that went south we later learned was headed for Washington, D.C. when it crashed in Pennsylvania. Can a vision get any closer than this?

Some who heard me speak of it came back to say they remembered my dream about New York City being terrorized by two eagles. All these years later, I am still haunted by this vision. When my then-wife Weasy saw it she said, "Oh my God Mutti!! Your dreams are coming true." It was there and then I realized that the things The Lord had been showing me were real. It was the ultimate confirmation substantiating an account that some would say was prophetic. Still, only time will tell of the things that I am now privy to. My question is, who would believe that I was also taken up into heaven?

Chapter 14
My First Vision & The Strange Visitation

Just before He showed me what was to take place on September 11, 2001, a day that would change the world forever, another strange event took place. I was in bed, and it was Sabbath night so the house was quiet. The kids were fast asleep—Richie in his room, in the front of the house, and the girls Tasha and Sabrina in the bedroom next to ours. I usually listened out for the girls if they were in their room playing when they were supposed to be sleeping, or Richie was a drawing his favorite cartoon characters, the Teenage Mutant Ninja turtles. Many a night, I'd gone into his room and turned off his light so that he could get his rest, for school the next day. But it was the Sabbath, so I was happy to be home in bed resting, with no need to wake up for work the next morning. I was in a deep sleep when something woke me up, though I didn't know what. Then the Spirit beckoned me to open my eyes, and I realized that there was a bright light in the room, which was quite strange indeed. My wife was beside me asleep, and I had turned off the light before going to bed that night. The light startled me, but I was more curious than anything else. As I wiped the sleep from my eyes, I still did not understand what or who was there, and as I lay there staring at this mysterious light that illuminated the room, I still could not get my mind and heart around this mystery. Is there an angel standing there? I thought to myself, as I moved slowly, wondering what on Gods earth could this mean. I followed the subtle brightness, and what I saw was more than breathtakingly mysterious, I must say. I followed the light to its source, and it was sitting right over the dresser above the mirror. At first I thought it was shining from outside, coming through the window. I lay there for a moment, and then got up and tiptoed, not wanting to wake Weasy up or disturb this strange occurrence. I looked out of the window, but all I could see was the beautiful night sky with the stars in their rightful places. Still, the light was hovering right above the dresser. What was most strange was that our room was on the second floor and located in the very back of the house. It overlooked a sizable grape vine that took up the entire driveway and back-yard laying right under our window, where at least three cars could park beneath it. It was a good sized house that we were renting at the time, and the kids were elated to be there because of the big back yard and the grape vine. It was in the middle of summer, so the vines were thick, with grapes hanging from all sides. Our children loved to climb up on the vines and sometimes on top of my car (though that got them into trouble) to pick the grapes. It was their playground and they loved it. I knew there was no way someone could have been outside shining a light through this window. The geometry would not allow it because of the thick grape vine covering most of the back yard. It would have had to be a helicopter or something hovering in the air and shining that light through our window, but there was no sound. And I don't believe in extraterrestrial life forms. As I stared at this mysterious beam of light, a perfect circle about a foot in diameter, fixed right above the dresser mirror, I wondered deeply what it could possible mean. The silence of the night was palpable.

My mind started making up all kinds of scenarios as I eased myself back into bed. It was baffling to lie there looking at the strange light with no one else in the room but my wife, and she was fast asleep. How would I tell her about this strange, unwavering light on the wall? I was doing everything in slow motion, not to disturb this phenomenon that transcended time and space. About a minute went by as I watched this startling light that lingered in this bright imperfect place in a perfect circle. I remained curious, as I pondered its meaning. With no more time to waste I shook Weasy awake to witness this strange marvel. As she startled out of her deep sleep, I pointed to the mirror for a moment without saying a word, to find out if she could see what I was witnessing. Not wanting to disturb whatever it was, I whispered "Can you see the light over the mirror?" But she said, "What are you talking about, Mutti?" I said in a low whispering tone, "Look … can't you see the bright light shining above the mirror?" She said again, "What light?" and then suddenly, it just vanished in the blink of an eye. Just like that.

It disappeared, as if someone in the room had turned off a switch. It had no beginning or ending and it didn't move one inch the whole time it was present. That was the amazing thing that it had never wavered or shifted for a second. One minute it was there, and the next minute it was gone. I ran back to the window to look at the sky because the light could not possibly have come from anywhere else. I looked everywhere outside from my window, but nothing was there. A strange occurrence indeed, but it was as real as night and day. This was not a dream but indeed an actuality. Did the Lord send one of His holy angels to enlighten me about the things to come, things that no one else will see? I guess only time will tell as you travel with me through the "black books of Moses, it secrets and last prophecies"

A Glimpse of Heaven and the Lion of Judah

Unable to go back to sleep, I remembered the very first mysterious dream and vision I'd had, a couple of years before this strange occurrence. I was standing in a strange, unrecognizable place when the spirit of The Lord beckoned to me to look up, and when I did, what I saw as I gazed into the sky was absolutely mind-boggling. I saw the clouds open up and roll back like an ancient scroll, and then the great mysterious doors of heavens opened up to my sinful mortal eyes. It was there that for the first time The Lord God of The Most High gave me a glimpse of heaven. I was astounded by what I saw and wondered what this could mean. Perhaps it was the new heaven and the new world that the Lord had promised to us. Or was it meant to tell me that, no matter what, knowing what was in our hearts before we did, and before the children had even found themselves, He would protect us as a family? I really don't know. But I was amazed to see all that The Lord showed me, or allowed me to witness. I saw beautiful fruits, trees, and flowers of many colors. And I saw a lush garden with beautiful animals, most noticeably a huge and powerful brown lion standing strong with great presence and beauty, his piercing eyes looking straight at me.

As I watched, I saw him walking to and fro in the heaven of heavens. I was not afraid of his presence because, though he looked powerful and mighty, there was a calmness about Him. I watched as the other animals walked near the lion and saw that they were not afraid or intimidated by him. There were many great things, more than my tongue could tell, because they were numerous and I only got a glimpse of them. In the midst of it all, I saw something profound and heart rendering. I saw my little family, (Weasy, myself, and the kids) sitting on a red couch having devotion and singing songs of praise to The Most High God. I was thrilled to see us in heaven, though I know my own sorrows and shortcomings, and that I am perfectly flawed. It was all surreal to me, and deep in my heart I knew I did not deserve to be there. My children and wife Weasy, yes! I could understand that, because I know Weasy loves the Lord and we were trying our best to raise the kids to honor, love, and revere The Most High God. But I know that my life was nowhere near worthy of heaven, as I struggled daily with my own demons that had their fangs in me, sucking my blood like vampires. And even when I fasted and prayed, I found myself going back to the same bed of sorrow. The place where great men lose their crown was the very place I found myself and almost lost mine and did lose my family, as no sin goes unpunished. But because I trust the Lord God of The Most High I know that I have to go through my different valleys of the shadow of death and cross many rivers to find Him again, and to be where He wants me to be. He has a plan for me, whether I have figured it out or not. All I know is that my heart always yearns after him and I deeply love Him and have always wanted to be among the ones who serve Him and to someday walk in righteousness on Earth. This was my greatest desire, to please Him and make him proud of me someday.

I couldn't continue to allow Lucifer to pull me down into the pits of hell, and so I held on to my Father, and He has never let go of me. He has always been merciful and kind to me, even in my darkest valley, gloomiest of hours and greatest despair. I have often found myself in a state of sadness and pain, in which I wept in silence more often than anyone could ever imagine. I wear my dark glasses always to hide the tears and the pain that lingers behind my smile and laughter. I ask The Lord daily for His everlasting mercies to be near me, undeserving though I am, and to please never let go of me even when I let go of Him. It is not my true will or desire to go astray, though I have often done so. But my guilt has weighed me down oftentimes, until I feel like I can hold on no longer. Overwhelmed by the heavy burden and the weight of sin, sometimes my hand slides from the Father's like on a slippery rope, but still I know he is there. No matter what, I feel His presence near me, though I am afraid to speak to Him sometimes because of my shame.

But one day, as I was walking through the park by myself, I decided to talk to Him to see if he would hear me or listen. I told him about my sorrows and the despair that comes from so many disappointments. And as I was telling him about my shame over having let Him down and that I don't deserve His mercies anymore, that's when He put His arms around me, and lifted me up and told me that He has never left me and that He is still my friend, and will always be to the end, if I want Him to be. What else could I do but break down and cry, thanking Him for His everlasting mercies and loving kindness that endure forever and forever. And then one day, when I least expected it, He set me free because my burden was gone from me and I felt free again. Today I tell you my stories so that someday soon, before it's eternally too late, you too can come and find Him (just as I have) to be kind and merciful and most of all loving and true. My testimonies and journey with the Lord would fill an entire library shelf if I should continue, but I will not bore you with all the details. I will tell you what The Lord God of The Most High has shown me over the years, and what He told me in the visions and dreams that were given to me. I was sent to you by The Lord God of The Most High, who not only showed me a glimpse of heaven, but also invited me to come up and spoke to me of many things, of which He said, "It is Time to tell it to you." It was 24 years ago that the visions started to come, and I did not understand them or even know why I was having them. My heart was full of questions: The Lord is showing me heaven? Me, who he knows to be so unworthy? At first it was not for me to speak of my heavenly encounters, because I thought that was for righteous men and women who have walked with God without sinning.

And I wouldn't want to run before the Lord, knowing my life to be so tainted and marred with sin. I hate hypocrisy with all my heart, so it was hard for me to speak of prophetic things. I can only speak of what He has done for me, of how kind and merciful He has been to me, undeserving though I am. What He has been showing me over the years I only told to my immediate family, but maybe I was being prepared for this moment in time. Just as Moses was exiled from Egypt after he committed murder and ended up in Median, in Jethro's, tent and for 40 years searched for his purpose on earth, so have I journeyed into the unknown of the mystery of The Lord God of heaven and earth.

The very first vision I had with the lion of Judah walking in the heavens, my wife Weasy was there in the vision, but strange indeed of what it all meant: As I found myself in this unknown place with Weasy, in an open field, as I gazed into the heaven of heavens with the windows of heaven still open like a scroll unfurled by the holy angels or a book opened by the hand of The Lord. I pointed to the heavens, awestruck and stunned by what I was seeing, and I put my arms around her shoulder, beckoning to her in the vision while I shook her physically in both Godly fear and excitement. I pointed with excitement for her to see this amazing Heavenly realm, but she only kept asking me, "What are you talking about Mutti!? What are you saying or trying to show me? Because I'm not seeing anything!" It was then I realized that she could not see what I was privy to, and no one would be able to because she was the closest to me and she couldn't. The Lord God of The Most high did not share the vision with her even though she was standing right beside me in the dream. Though she was a God-fearing woman, she could not see what I was seeing. Then it hit me that what I had just seen would be the beginning of a mysterious illuminous path, my personal and spiritual journey to the mountain of the Most High

God, filled with many hills and more valleys than I could ever imagine, all of which I must overcome to arrive where The Lord intends to bring me. The Most High showed me many things, and there would be many more to come if I stayed on the path of righteousness. As the Lord said, "Only those who are faithful unto the end shall be saved." I have to stay faithful for God's sake and if I ever want to see this New Jerusalem that He has given me glimpses of. On this uncharted journey, only a few will believe what I am about to tell you of the things that were shown to me in visions and dreams. I pray that you will be among those who believe.

Chapter 15

It's Not about Religion, But the Relationship with God

Have No Fear of The Hateful Child

In the rise of the tribulation president, you must have no fear of the hateful child that will come to you with a smile. I must warn you that he is coming, and many will be deceived by him, if The Lord God does not shorten the time for the sake of the elect. It's not going to be pretty I must say, God help us, or else we all will be deceived. I am so unworthy of life itself much-less God's love. And unworthy as I am, I ask your forgiveness as well for being so late in my delivery, still I hope it's not too late in telling you what I was given to give to you, if you wish to hear. I've been given a second chance by The Lord to come and tell you, of the many things I have seen, and is still been privy to as the windows of heaven keep opening and The Lord gives me little glimpses of tomorrow. Some of the things I was shown and what I was told often blows my mind but it's not for me to decide so here I am. It's going to be up to you now from here onward.

I was not sent to convert you or to condemn you, but only to tell you, or remind you if you already know, again you don't have to believe. You have the choice, to choose and I can tell you this that any person, or church, or organization of any kind or religion that tries to force you to serve God The Most High is not of Him and was not sent by Him because The Lord God has never forced anyone to serve Him. He gave us freedom of choice, the greatest gift ever given to mankind. The Lord God does not need man's "help!" He will not accept force love, and could not, because it's against His character. Think of this for a moment "God The Most High forcing man to serve Him or you kidding me! Who do we believe God is for Him to want man, to force another man to serve Him? Isn't this a bit strange, when all things belong to Him, knowing that He is God and God Alone, and He could make us as robots if that was His intention, instead of giving us as humans the freedom of choice? Don't be fooled by these snakes and wolves camouflaged in the deepest deception and acting like shepherds of God when they are really agents of their father, the devil. (Wolves in sheep clothing)

Can a man help or judge God the Most High, whose ways are as far as the East is from the West in comparison to the fallible minds of men? Who is man that God should be mindful of him? Is there any comparison to the infinite wisdom of The Most High God? Many will come in His name and will try to force worship upon you. This you must know is not of God, and will be a sign to you that you are dealing with the antichrist. It doesn't matter how pious they look or claim to be. Don't be fooled by their beautiful and deadly camouflage smiles covered in great deception. Whether it's Catholicism, or any other religious sect including Islam or any other form of Christianity, Judaism it doesn't matter, you must not believe them, when they come knocking on your door, which will be sooner than you, may think. You'll be threatened with death as usual, which is the ultimate punishment if you don't comply, with worshiping the beast that is to come (if he is not already here by the time you read these words), but still you must not believe them, it's a hoax.

The secret behind the secret of Satan's strategy is force and fear mixed with the threat of death. Well I'm here to tell you, have no fear! God will force no man to serve Him or worship Him, but remember this: He protects His own—those who choose to serve

Him out of love and love only, and only those who seek him will find Him. He told us, "If you love me keep my commandment." It's we who need Him (The Savior of The world), not the other way around. On the other hand, it's Satan who wants to see us dead. While The Lord God want to save us from ourselves, and bless us with eternal life as the life giver, with freedom of choice to choose the light over the darkness. What can the devil do for you but cause you much more pain and despair, fill with much heartache? What is there in this wicked monster devil that is attractive, that men should trade their souls for? This is food for thought. Think it through thoroughly before making any decision that you will regret eternally. We are consumed by sin because we choose to disobey God, deceived and seduced by this serpent whose wicked desire and intention is to see each and every one of us lose our eternal soul. He is not partial in his revenge against us. He wants to see us all in hell with him, begging God for our lives when it is forever too late. Lucifer hates his Creator and hates himself even more. When he realized that what he had instigated long before this world was created had back-fired. The power he thinks he has had got him kicked out of the kingdom of God. Today he runs around like a spoil lost child with wicked and spiteful intention to corrupt Gods children, just like what he did in heaven corrupting Gods holy angels. But his plan did not worked out as he thought it would. Reason is that Lucifer is an illusionist believing that he can do things that he cannot, because The Most High had given him a little taste of power in heaven, and it got to his head and he thought he had it all, just to be reminded that he is only a created being. This is what power does, it changes you as a person if you don't know God The Most High, and absolute power corrupts as it has corrupted many men on earth who have ended up on the dump heaps of history. Just think if the eternal-code was not in place, what chaos this world would be, with Lucifer at the helm?

He hates you so much more than you would ever believe, and every moment of the day he thinks about killing you, and if he could he would. But he cannot unless The Most High God gives him the green light to do so. The secret behind the secret is that he wants you to burn in hell because he also hates you. He hates you because God has created us in His own image, to take the places of the angels who rebelled against Him—Lucifer and his followers who got kicked out of heaven. The secret behind the secret is that the promise The Lord God of The Most High made to Abraham as the father of many nation, as his descendant……….will be like the sand of the sea and like the stars in the sky is the replacement of the angels who have rebel against The Most High God. What you and I refuse to understand is that He is a God of order, and nothing that He has done is a coincident. You and I have a chance to see God The Most High in His glory and splendor. It will make you wonder how Satan could be stupid enough to give up the beauty and splendor of heaven. He seeks vengeance against us for inheriting the love and mercy and generosity of God that was once his. He is like a spoiled hateful child determined to make sure that no one else can have what he can't. This is the true nature of who we are dealing with.

When I was sent back to Earth,(which you will find in one of the greatest visions, when I was taken up into heaven) the first thing the Lord showed me (on returning to earth) was a bunch of teenagers having much fun. They were all lined up to go see a movie, and what I was told by The Lord to do still baffles me. You'll find the vision in "Invited to Heaven - to Speak to The Lord God of The Most High." Stunning and unbelievable that He would invite someone like me, perfectly flawed to come into his holy presence, and He speak to me like a friend or a father and a son. You'll find this vision in volume 2 of the chronicles "**We All Have Been**

Deceived".

Lucifer is stealing our precious little children through creeping compromise, through the subliminal messages hidden in the honeycomb of pop culture, through the internet and social media, disrespecting The Most High's righteous and holy name, in the derogatory and distasteful lyrics of the music they listen to, and we as parents are allowing it to happen. The truth of the matter is that most of these kids do not know the truth because we're so busy running down the world and the god of money, that we've missed out on the opportunity to spend quality time with them and to build foundation by instilling the word of God in their little hearts. If we do not teach them, how do we expect them to learn about Him? Music and many of the films today, has instigated rebellion against The Most High God in so many cases, dishonoring His righteous and Holy Name in blasphemous subliminal connotation, when He should be honored, loved, and exalted. And that's not to mention The Ancient of Days whose infinite love and glory are beyond the limited vocabulary of man's intellectual capacity to describe. I'll give you a little glimpse of the atrocity of the young people that Lucifer pulls under the water every day, like a hungry alligator that has no limits in its quest and taste for blood.

The secret behind the secret is that worldwide one person commits suicide every 40 seconds. And who gets the glory? Nobody but Lucifer, because this is what he does best—bring you into the pits of hell by bringing you into the depths of the greatest state of depression, poverty, and stress, through peer pressure and pride. This is the place where so many young people lose the fight and eventually their crown, because they lack the knowledge of The Lord God of The Most High that would enable them to deal with the curve balls that life bring you. And as always, Lucifer shows you the easy way out, instead of the struggle through the fire that great men and women have gone through to become stalwarts for the Lord, able to inspire many around the world.

Who Am I?

You may be asking who am I (and what authority I speak with), well let me tell you a little about myself and it is with humility of heart I speak in such humble, unassuming tone, without a doubt undeserving of such spiritual encounters in no uncertain terms. The Only Begotten of The Most High invited me to come up into His holy mountain in a vision and let me know that I was from the tribe of Levi, though I had been lost in the rubble of Jamaica most of my life and have struggled to find myself, knowing that something was deeply wrong as my soul longed after Him and to be perfectly whole. Was I wrong to feel this way? I make no apology whatsoever for having felt what I feel ever since I was a boy, and I would never trade my struggle for anything in the world, as it has helped make me who I am.

I was also invited into heaven to meet with the Lord God of The Most High which was the greatest of all of the visions I have received. It's the greatest experience any mortal soul can experience. I have been taken in the spirit to many places, which is so different from flying from places to places in dreams and visions. I was told many things, from the mouth of The Lord God Himself, when I was invited into heaven. When I was there, He reveal to me things that I don't even understand myself, it was so much I could not retain it all, reason is I was more in disbelief, shocked of what I was seeing and what I was hearing, from the lips of The Lord God of The Most High Himself. But the mystery within a mystery was the day I heard His great and mighty Majestic and mysterious voice speak to me in real time. Out of the heavens of heavens He called me by my name. This is what has sealed my faith in The God of my fathers, knowing that He has been my friend all along, much longer than this specific day that has put in my heart the spiritual-blueprint of my journey of which I had no clue would have taken so many slippery slopes. but I have loved him all my life as I have known He has loved me. The truth of the matter is that I have loved Him ever since I knew myself, because I realized that He has loved me long before I was born and long before my mother and grandmother was. I thought just been told by The Lord Himself that I was from the tribe of Levi was enough to know, when I thought these things were unheard of in our modern world. Levi was the third child of Israel, and Judah was the fourth and most powerful, which is why the number four is the most prophetic number of all, causing prophetic changes and spiritual chaos ever since the creation of Earth.

It was the lineage of the fourth son of Israel that would culminate in The Christ Child. It was the fourth commandment of God that we keep holy the day on which He rested, after creating the heavens and earth in six days, calling the seventh day the holy Sabbath. It is through obedience, not force that we keep the Sabbath holy, because God will not accept force, only love. Obedience has to come directly from the heart. The secret behind the secret is that many things that was told to me in heaven that I could not remember, is now reveal to me each day as The Spirit of God speak to my mind as I write these chronicles, with humility of heart and spirit. The mystery of my journey is in the visions and dreams that were given to me, if you should put them all together you might find something that you'll never believe in these four chronicles that I was given the assignment to write. I will tell you this little secret which is not a secret but is hidden and will only be revealed to those who are prospective citizens of heaven: The key to the kingdom of heaven is hidden in the parables. Those who will be saved will search for them, they will not depend on pastors and priest and bishops to tell them, they'll search the scriptures for themselves. If you cannot read buy the bible in audio and rewind it until you find it. It's the only way you will protect yourself from being deceived, which will bring down both rich and poor free and bond.

****

This very timely premonition was given to me for His own reason that I could never question, because He is God and God alone, and I am humbled to be His servant. My biggest fear was not delivering the message in a timely manner, and I would never want to be seen as incompetent by The Lord God of the Most High because many are called but only a few are chosen. If this is my only reason for coming to Earth, then I pray that I have done His will, and that if I have been faithful in carrying out His instruction, I pray that you too will be blessed by what I have told you if you choose to believe. If you receive these messages after you finish reading these books, and whatever decision you make consciously because of the information you will receive, then my life on Earth would not be in vain. I know that the timing is the essential factor in prophecy and was hoping my words wouldn't influence anyone's vote, because what I was given has no political inclination to it, as in Luke 20:25: "Give unto Caesar the things that are Caesar's and unto God the things that are God's." This is much bigger than any political arena in the most powerful country on Earth, the things I was made privy to.

I hate politics, though it is a necessary evil. Without it, what kind of chaos would be in the world, though it helps to create some of the chaos itself. It couldn't be otherwise with powerful opponents in every political arena in the world, all worshipping their own egos. But it was meant to be this way, and will always be as long as Lucifer, the prince of darkness, still roams the world with his thug angels, fallen from grace. They were created with the same freedom of choice that you and I have, but they chose to trade theirs in by rebelling against The Most High. Lucifer started this rebellion in heaven, and it got him thrown out of heaven corrupting Gods holy angels with his serpent tongues of lies, hate and deceit, which will surely cause him eternal damnation in the end. There are severe consequences from choosing to go against the laws that the Most High put in place to govern His universe. The greatest thing behind the secret is that you and I still stand a chance to make it into the kingdom of God if we are faithful unto the end of our existence on Earth, not forgetting that our redemption comes when we breathe our last breath. Ignorance of God's laws is no excuse, but because His love is more powerful than His anger, the intent of our hearts becomes paramount, and you and I will be judged accordingly. —that you and I might have a chance to live forever if we are faithful, while he has blown his chance at eternal life.

Chapter 16

I Was Shown Nebuchadnezzar's Dream in a Vision

This Time the Statue Turns Up-Side down...... What on God's Earth Is This?

I had a very disturbing dream and vision in one, never before seen anything like this that must be made known to the world before it's eternally too late. This is no ordinary dream and must not be taken lightly. Once I give it to you what is to come upon us as a people will not be on my shoulders. Only Yashua The Christ will be able to bring everlasting peace to the world, and before this, total destruction is the only solution. "There is a God in heaven who reveals secrets and makes known what shall be in the latter days" (Daniel 2:28). This vision came to me near the end of December, 2011. It was the end of the year, so I was looking forward to a new year with different possibilities. I was on the verge of a new beginning and was home, mostly fasting and praying. I spent much of my time in meditation. I just wanted some answers because I had too many unanswered questions. It was during my very first 21-day fast, when I took some time off to finish writing a book entitled, "The Manifestation of a Spiritual and Conscious Revolution." I simply wanted some direction from The Most High.

This particular night, I went to bed, and during a deep sleep I was made privy to end time events that were yet to come, and it disturbed me greatly. I was given this vision in the middle of the night, and as I was in vision I saw a place I had never been or seen before. I was out in the open, in a strange place in the middle of the day. The sun was shining, and the sky was as beautiful as ever— the perfect day for a family picnic, with just a few cirrus cloud puffs scattered across the sky. I found myself with my sister Veronica, who lives in Canada, was working with me on a huge unfinished house.

It seemed in the vision as if the house belonged to her or someone close to her, and I was only there to give her a hand. When I looked around all that was visible was the foundation of the house, which was a very good size. I was in the process of laying down some bricks, or building blocks to be accurate. It was then that I heard the sound of a motor in the distance, and out of the blue a good friend of mine rode up on a motorcycle. It was an old friend that I hadn't seen in years, and I was elated to see him. He was the bass player from my old band (half Scottish and part English), whom I had nicknamed Carlo— one of the coolest brothers ever.

I stopped what I was doing and went to chat with him for a moment, and as always we started talking and laughing about old times in the band, stretching back twenty years. He was there for a while, and with him were a couple more people scattered around the yard, and perhaps one or two of my daughters, but since I couldn't tell which ones, I guess their presence was not very significant in this vision (otherwise I would remember clearly). As we were talking, I realized that the reason Carlo came looking for me was that he wanted me to go somewhere with him. I told him that I couldn't, despite how hard he tried to convince me. I had to tell him that I would be spending the rest of the day giving my sister a hand. We had to finish the foundation of this huge house that we were helping to build so that the rest of the builders could start their work, it seemed. I recall Carlo standing there still trying to get me to leave with him on his journey, and the truth of the matter is that he was very persuasive.

I almost went, but something told me not to, and as always, I listened to that still small voice that speaks wisdom to my heart and my mind and I did listen. As I stood there talking to my friend, the Spirit of The Lord God of The Most High spoke to me in that same little small voice that told me gently to look up. As soon as I looked up to the sky, something caught my eye. I noticed that there was a star in the sky that was visible in the middle of the day. It was bigger than normal, which was peculiar (because only the moon can be seen in the early morning when the dawn breaks, and it departs with the rising sun). For some reason, this lonely star was standing in the heavens by itself. My curiosity deepened as I looked upon it in wonder. I realized that it was to the East of where I was standing. Suddenly, I noticed some strange wonders or revelations as they were happening. What could this possible mean, I asked myself as I gazed in awe, oblivious of Carlos' presence. The things taking place in the sky I had never seen before! They were happening right in front of my eyes, and I was in wonderment!

What I saw next was frightening and terrifying to behold. Sparks started shooting from the star in every direction. Sparks shot out in a straight line, which made it look as if there were two stars beside each other. The first star resembled a star that that I had been watching for a year through my window around the same time of the vision. As the Spirit of The Lord beckoned to me to keep looking and witness the salvation of Almighty God, my eyes fixed on the revelation of what is to come. Out of nowhere, a patch of dark gray clouds crept in like a veil, covering the star momentarily. The Spirit of The Most High beckoned to me to keep looking, and I stared in great amazement as the sight in the sky gradually became more terrifying. The benign beginning of the vision could not prepare me for what this possibly could mean. It resembled the beginning of the end of the world as we know it. It was as if the apocalypse had begun, because the most alarming and startling things were taking place. The sky scrolled back, and the heavens opened! What I saw next was as devastating as it was astonishing. I saw a huge golden image of a man with folded arms, like the one in Nebuchadnezzar's dream, which he could neither remember nor explain. Fortunately for Nebuchadnezzar, the prophet Daniel reiterated what he saw and also gave him the interpretation thereof.

Could this be what I was seeing? It seemed to be of the same magnitude as the very same image described in the book of Daniel but without the partitions. This seemed impossible. Had it not taken up the entire window of heaven that was made open to me, I would have thought that I was looking at the miniature statues that Hollywood awards actors and actresses at the Oscars. I initially thought this great image resembled those little gold statuettes, except that it was much too big. What made this even more intriguing and mysterious is that the image was golden while the back ground was black and white, as is usual in my visions.

After the appearance of this big golden image another mysterious figure appeared in the sky. This time a scroll in the heavens I saw a scroll pass before me, and what came next was another mystery within a mystery. I started seeing things of the world, cities and buildings, countries, and men of renown. Event after event rolled out rapidly before my eyes, one after the other, so quickly that I could not identify them. I wasn't able to keep up with every one of the soon forgotten images, because they were many and fast-paced, and lacking specific detail.

The frightening appearance of the scroll made me fearful of what might come next and ended my speculation as to what the golden statue image represented. I didn't want to believe it, but as I stared in amazement I realized that I could not dismiss the revelatory similarities between what I thought Nebuchadnezzar and Daniel could have seen. As the scroll was winding out to whatever mysterious thing was to come next, something else happened. The huge golden image that once filled the entire window of heaven came back into view and now seemed to be counting down to something strange and even more mysterious. Then it suddenly started spinning rapidly as I gazed in astonishment. It appeared to be spinning out of control, so fast it made my head spin, and I had to keep moving my head to keep up with the consecutive events rapidly playing out. Even today, I'm dumbfounded and still cannot understand its meaning.

Everything except for the statue resembled a documentary on the book of Revelation, the premiere source of information about the events of the last days. I asked myself what this could possibly mean. The big golden human statue/image that stood with its arms folded when the heavens were scrolled back and I got my second glimpse into heaven had me totally stunned. I may not have known what I was witnessing when it all began, but I realized now that I was seeing the events and images of things to come. I also realized that they will be happening so fast that we won't be able to keep up with them. Will you and I be ready for the things I saw next? I was stunned, and I'm still astonished, because I know that many will not believe that what The Lord God of The Most High showed me is fast approaching. God help us!! I could not tell what the different parts of the statue represented, because I was not privy to those details, and I guess it's not really necessary for the Lord God of Heaven and Earth to have shown me and again. It would have been irrelevant, anyway, after what I saw next. The movement of the statue came to a slow, screeching and rapid halt. This was making sounds in the heavens I have never heard before, scary and mysterious. As it stopped, it turned in slow motion as if in another dimension, until it was upside down, with its feet upward in the air and its head towards the ground. What made it mysterious and mystical is that it was attached to nothing. It was spinning between time and space, as if it was being made to move by an unseen hand. I watched in awe and intense adoration, wondering what I would see next and hoping to get some indication as to what this could possibly mean.

In a matter of seconds after the spinning stopped, the figure paused for a moment as I gazed into the heavens with cringing anticipation, with my heart pounding in disbelief. I stood in amazement, as if an unseen time-clock was counting off something in slow motion—1, then 2, then 3, and then a pause, and then 4— and then all of a sudden all hell burst loose. My heart was beating wildly, triggering the panic mode in my mind, and as I stared into the Heavens in total shock, what I saw next was more than tongue can tell. I cringed in disbelief, and my heart was beating out of rhythm. I wanted to close my eyes, but I couldn't, and I put my hand on my head in Godly fear as if I knew something devastating was about to happen. And I don't know why, but in my guts I knew this was it.

Then I heard the greatest explosions of lightning and thunder and the sky lit up with bomb after bomb as the wars of the world began. The curtains of heaven unveiled its windows to my sinful, mortal, unworthy eyes while the heavens lit up with explosion after explosion of nuclear proportions shook the heavens and the visions of war obliterated the gray sky as the earth shook from the effect of the devastation I was witnessing. Though I had no idea of what the Lord was showing me, I did not know for certain or understand it, because no words were spoken to me in my mind, which is how The Lord usually communicated with me. I stared up into the clouds through the open window that made heaven visible to me, and I could see devastation in every direction. Explosion after explosion, atomic bombs were shooting from out of the earth at rapid speed, and they were coming from everywhere, like nothing you could imagine. The world was at war and the sky lit up in the middle of the day, not from lightning and thunder out of Heaven, but rather from hell on Earth. Chaos roiled in the clouds, raining terror on the world through the open window like nothing we've seen before, until the scroll was slowly rolled back.

These flashes in the heavens streaking across the sky from a place behind the clouds were traumatizing. Even after the windows of heaven were closed the scroll of clouds rolling back there were still explosions going on as I could hear the heavens in turmoil. With each explosion, a question exploded in my mind. Is this the cycle of world events prophesied to usher in the Antichrist, the last moment in time to the end of the world, as we know it? The perfect platform to echo world peace and he would be the one to suffice such eminent and important order for humankind. Can't you see where we are heading , but then again it will be The Most High who will decide what was shown to me.

The most significant part of the dream happened when I beckoned to Veronica and Carlo. I asked them if they had seen what I had just seen. For once, the answer was different. They both said, "yes!" I was astonished when I heard them say "We saw it!!" I said to myself "Wow!! This indeed is really the end!" Usually when the Lord is showing me Heavenly apocalyptic things, no one around can see it, though they might be standing right beside me. So this vision within a dream was a bit different from all of the rest. It started off as a dream that led to a vision.

With astonishment at the great and wicked day ahead, I solemnly bowed my head in great despair. Of this great tribulation the Lord said, "If it was possible, even the very elect of God would be lost." Again as I was standing gazing into the heavens I then saw the heavenly scroll roll back slowly as if the hand of God pulled the curtains and closes back up the windows of heaven, and I awoke out of the vision.

My Interpretation—Could It Be Right or Wrong?

In the vision, I didn't know what to look for, because many, many things were happening in a very brief time. For some reason, I cannot recall all that I saw on the scroll, as it went by me rapidly and there were too many events competing for my attention. But one thing I remember is that before the great catastrophe I could see people walking in a busy street, shopping and just walking casually, some doing window shopping, many with faces I recognized as men of renown. Oh my Lord!! It was crazy to behold. Was I not meant to understand everything I saw? The truth of the matter is that I really did not know what I was witnessing. Everything that is going to happen before the end of time will happen so quickly that our heads will be spinning in disbelief of the horrors that will engulf the world. What was surprising to me is that The Lord had also been showing me a star that reminded me of the vision. For a month I sat in my bedroom window at 135 Hawthorne Street in Bridgeport, Connecticut and watched it, trying to make sense out of this bright star that appeared every evening, in the same spot. Because the stars in the vision brought my attention to this particular star, I went to the CNN website and searched to see if any of the newscasters or pundits were speaking about this one star that stood out from all the rest. It was in the north but was positioned lower than any star that I've ever seen. Whatever time the sun went down, that one star appeared first due to its brightness. As a matter of fact, I saw this same low hanging star in the twilight hours of the morning as I was writing about this very vision. There was a new day on the Horizon; 2011 was gone forever and 2012 was now here—the year when it was said the world would end according to the Mayan calendar.

One thing that was significant in this vision is that one of my daughters, who was in her early twenties, was there, with some of her friends. This is very, very significant as I believe they will be around as young adults to witness this wicked and grave atrocity that is about to come upon mankind when it arrives, which means that it will be in this time when all of this will be fulfilled. The other thing that was very strange was that Veronica and Carlo witnessed everything with me, as if to say this is really the final countdown in earth's history, and everyone will see all that is to come. How many will live to tell the story? That I don't know. The secret behind the secret is that this very star seems to me to be the one that heralded Jesus Christ's birth 2,015 years ago, though only a few wise men would understand what it meant at the time. And I've seen it in several visions that are more than a mystery to me. My question is, why does The Lord God of The Most High keep showing this very star to me? I'm not the only one who has noticed this star. Another brother by the name of Josh has been studying the movements of this star, and I know that many wise men and women around the world have noticed it. I have pointed it out to a couple of my brethren, including Charlie (Genna) and Legend (Nigel), and they both told me that it was not real, couldn't be real. I showed it to my wife, Dorr, and my kids, and they also found it hard at first to believe that it was real. I was brought to its awareness by The Spirit of The Most High in the very time I was on Hawthorne Street by myself in fasting and prayer. We may not understand what is about to happen, but these signs of the time are upon us.

TRUMP THE NEBUCHADNEZZAR of TODAY

This Nebuchadnezzar statue is the most significant piece of prophetic evidence that the world has come to its final spin, counting down to a screeching deadly and wicked halt. The men that The Lord God of heaven and earth tasks with finishing the world are appointed by Him for these trying days that will come. President Trump will dictate to the rest of the world all of the laws that will govern the nations, and they will implement them for the sense of security that they mistakenly think they will gain. Under these very laws, the tone of the new world order will be set in stone until the final countdown. President Donald Trump is the Nebuchadnezzar of today, who will bring to fruition the great prophecy of Daniel 2.

What you must never forget (those who understand bible prophecy) is that Nebuchadnezzar passed the power to his son Belshazzar before the prophecy of Isaiah came to pass. This you must research for yourself, to understand the great omen that hovers over our heads, making this moment in time the most dangerous in the history of the world.

America will be the last power on earth and will hand the power to the beast. But this baton will be passed to someone younger than himself to be handed to the beast. The fact that my sister and brethren were able to see what I was seeing as it was happening simply means that all the players who are supposed to inflict the last blow on the face of the earth are already in place. What we must never forget is that the fourth kingdom, which never dies, is

Rome and that everything needed to accomplish its goals has already been put in place. President Trump will show his true colors, and when a man tells you who he is, you must believe him. He has already told the American people who he is, though some don't want to believe. All they are seeing is dollar signs because they believe that candidate Trump will be able to shake the money tree of America. The fourth beast will be more dreadful and terrible than before and after his deadly wound has healed he will be coming with a vengeance that no man on the face of the earth has seen before.

There won't be any rebellion or protest against the power of the Jesuits on earth this time. There have been those in every generation who believed that the end is near, but it has never happened. The wicked truth is that it is no longer a myth. The end is here, and you will see it for yourself. Nebuchadnezzar never saw the statue turned upside down. This is what was shown to me in vision, and it means that it is finished. I don't know much about prophecy and will never represent myself as a bible scholar. What I know is what was given to me to give to you. It is finished, my friends. Donald Trump said he will make sure that the Catholic church get its respect in America. Truth of the matter is that every church has equal respect in America, what he really means is that the catholic church will regain its power this time in America.

Don't take my word for it, time has a way of telling all of the untold stories that are lurking in the dark It will be up to you to decide what this is all about. They will call unholy holy and the holy things of The Most High God unholy. Welcome to the great tribulation. Whenever we see men doing things that we have never seen before, they call it demonic, but the devil and I can never be friends because I am a child of the One who sent me. If I tell you that Donald Trump will be the man to disarm America of the 2nd amendment, you are going to laugh at me, and call me a fool.

This which the Democrats have so often been accused of trying to do, well it's not going to be them it's the other way around. The tribulation president is the one who is ordained to do such, as I believe will start at the end of 2017 ,get ready for the beginning of the end. America is getting ready to do things un-American. You will give up your guns willingly, exchanging it for a false security and those who refuses will pay with their lives. The New world Order cannot be implemented with guns in civilian hands. So sit back and watch the new normal in action. If you think I'm crazy, you don't have to take my word for it. Just watch and see for yourself, at least I have told you so. I often wonder why I am one of them , chosen to tell you all of this ,that most of you really don't want to hear , I'm sorry if you're one of them, but I'm compelled to do so. Please don't take this premonition for granted, this statue that Nebuchadnezzar was shown ,was one of the greatest breakthrough of where the world was heading and if scientist would have studied the bible then instead of leaning to their own understanding ,man would be in a better position to deal with what is to come. Today or 4 years ago to be exact I was shown the very same golden image in the heavens of heaven and I have kept it a secret trying to figure it all out on my own until The Lord told me in another vision that it is now time to tell you all the things that He has been showing or privy me to.

These little glimpses of tomorrow is mighty frightening . I pray that you will understand the importance of what I have seen and what it really meant. I cannot warn you enough , this is the end of the world as we know it you're going to be amazed of the many events after events that is going to blow your mind. Things that you'll never be able to wrap your mind around, when you see these things started happening, the ones that make no sense to you , you must know that the TIME is here, yes you're there ,if I'm not around to see it. It's going to creep upon us without any announcement. The writing on the walls of Babylon was rapid. There was no time to think and then comes the end.

This powerful golden image that I was privy to turned upside down in the heavens taking up the entire window of heaven. It was after this that everything changed and the world was at a place that we'd never seen before. I pray that these world leaders Trump/Pence, Putin, and China premier will know what we're up against, God help us!!

The Mystical Encounter of the Burning Candle

And in this time, I would have devotion in the evening to bring in the Sabbath and would light three candles in a stand made of brass, in front of the fireplace in my living room, and put four little ones on the floor to make it seven. As I would light the three candles on the stand plus the other four little ones on the ground to commemorate the Holy Sabbath, and also to represent the 7 candlestick that was in the temple of The Most High God. I would sit with my guitar and sing songs of praise to The Lord God of the Most High, in solemn adoration of His love and mercy towards me and my family, a man drenched in sin and clothed in iniquity.

My intent was to bring my sins to the foot of the cross at my Savior's feet ,as I had learned as a boy by watching my mother ever fighting the enemy on her knees, in great pain and supplication. It was how I learned to take my burdens to the feet of The Most High, and as often as I do so in great supplication and humility of heart, He shows His presence in different ways. Sometimes as I sing and pray, His presence (In The spirit of The Holy

Spirit) comes near me and consumed me, often throwing me to the ground, where I cannot make a sound. Sometimes it lasts for seconds, sometimes maybe minutes or more. Sometimes He makes His presence clear to me in the candles that I light to bring in the holy Sabbath, with the one in the middle shining brighter than the others. The first time it happened, I thought it was not real. But as time went by, and I sang songs like

> "Under His wings I am safely abiding, there I find comfort and there I am blessed, often when earth has no balm for my healing, still I can trust Him for I am His child,"

the middle candle would often flare up in a solemn mystical flame, supernatural and transcendent and as real as the daylight outside and the sun that sets on the beautiful shores around the world.

These are the things that solidify my personal relationship with my Lord, who to me is The Lord God of The Most High, the only Begotten of The Ancient of Days. He has been my friend ever since I was a little boy. At the very tender age of about seven, I would go into the woods behind my house and speak to him, and He would speak back to my heart and my mind. I have always known that He was there, but never knew how much He cares for me. I am humbled, and in humility of heart and solemn and great adoration of the One who sent me, I write these words for you. My daughter Sabrina witnessed this strange mystical and sacred phenomenon one Sabbath evening when she came and worshipped with me. I welcome witnesses to what the Lord is showing me in visions and dreams, and the mystical and supernatural snips of things I get glimpses of every now and then, too surreal sometimes to share. Some of them are for my eyes only and come to strengthen my faith, and sometimes test it. I was able to capture one or two of the supernatural events on my phone, though I did not want to disturb such a spiritual and holy encounter. But I guessed that if the Lord wanted me to show it to you, the candle would stay in its supernatural state and if not, I would not be able to capture it in a photograph/video. I was able to get a good picture of the flaring middle candle, just that you may believe. I got a couple shots of such occurrences, so that someday you might be able to see it for yourself. One day I will put the images on my website, TheBlackBooksofMoses.com or on YouTube. When you see the images, you can be the judge. It will be up to you to believe, or not to believe. I can only show what was shown to me, and tell you what I have seen in dreams and visions. I only do this because I know that the TIME IS NOW!! And we are all guilty of procrastination, which is the stealer of time and our eternal soul. It is in this moment that was prophesied by Daniel that the stone that was cut out of the sky without hands came out of nowhere from the East and struck the image of silver and gold, bronze and iron, and to the very most venerable place and time in history, the feet of iron and clay taking it down to the ground in a mighty crash, mincing it into dust that was blown away in the wind, never to return. The Most High God of heaven and earth will set up a kingdom that shall never be broken. You must know how it will happen and what it will be, so you won't be deceived as even the very elect of God would be if He does not shorten the days.

Chapter 17

Americans Will Vote with Their Hearts & Not Their Conscience

"Who Can Blamed Them ......When They Think That The White Race Is In DANGER!!"

The Jesuits Closer to the Throne of America Than ever?

The election of 2016 was not about the Republican Party but rather about Donald Trump. I predicted months earlier that this time America would vote with their hearts rather than their conscience because so many felt left out in the cold. Their feeling that everything was slipping away from them intensified with the election of Barrack Obama, the 44th president of the United States of America and our first black president. (Bear in mind the significance of the number 4, and that 44 means prophetic changes.) Puzzled, frustrated, and disagreeing with changes they didn't understand, they need to take back control at whatever price and by whatever means necessary, even if that meant voting for a candidate Trump, a man who did not embody their conservative ideals. They saw Trump as the one who could restore what they felt they had lost even if that meant voting against their conscience.

If they were not convinced of Trump's opposition to abortion and gay-marriage, they were willing to overlook that because feeling like an outsider doesn't sit well with millions of white Americans who viewed President Obama as unacceptably liberal (and for many, unacceptably black). For many of them, Obama, despite his accomplishments, will go down in history as one of the worst presidents because of his liberal stands against their conservative ideals, and they saw electing Hilary Clinton as a continuation of the Obama administration. That's the way the pundits will explain Trump's unexpected victory. The real truth is that Donald trump will be the tribulation president for the final countdown of earth's history. The great tribulation must last for seven years and will more or less commemorate in 2018 the 70th anniversary of the rebirth of Israel.

The beginning of the end commences with the great tribulation and this monster (the creeping compromise of the American experience) that we as a people have created and now will not be able to control will take precedent deep in the American fabric. President Trump will not be working from his own instinct, but at the direction of the powers that be, powers that he himself will not be able to control, though he will be a willing participant in what is about to come upon us as a nation and upon the entire world. Whether he will live out his presidency or be impeached or resign, I really don't know, but what I was made privy to by the Spirit of The Most High is that the vice president will play a major role in the final transfer of power to the beast of Revelation 13 in the year 2024 which would culminate the great tribulation. Where we go from here I really don't know either, but I'll wait upon the Lord for the answer.

Chapter 18

Is Vice President Mike Pence The Mystery Man In The Puzzle?

Who is Mike Pence the Mystery Man in the Puzzle?

Is Mike Pence the one ordained to hand the baton to the beast of Revelation 13, the Catholic church? In Revelation 13, The Lord also shows me something very, very significant, which is never to be taken lightly but must be looked into with a second glance. And it's what tells me that Vice President Mike Pence, in the perfect storm, will play the key role in the final countdown of this presidency during the great tribulation. Don't take my word for it. You shall see. What you must understand in this moment in time is that man has no control over the events that are to come. We are all merely players or participants in this mysterious puzzle of life. The secret behind the secret is that we decide as individuals what we will become in life long before we reach our teenage years. Our situation usually dictates how far we will go. Some are born privileged while others are born into great adversity, like those who are born in the ghettoes of the world, and should never feel bad about their humble beginning because they do not chose the ghetto; it's the ghetto that chooses them. We have no choice over who our parents are. Can a child choose to be born into poverty or as the child of a wealthy person? The answer is no, not at all! Not one of us has any control over where we're placed on life's journey.

It is these factors that decide who and what we will become and how far we will go—physically, emotionally, and financially in a society that caters to the elites who set the tone for the rat-race they have created, where chasing after an illusion is the design to divert us from the spiritual aspect of our lives. This has become the core ideology of our society today. The motto is "get rich, or die trying." Spirituality is a totally different kettle of fish, as the spiritual and the physical live in two different worlds. Our surroundings are a key factor in determining the choices we will make in life. How many children of wealth and privilege end up on drugs, living immoral lives? And how many children born into crushing poverty end up among the elite, making decisions as to whether those privileged ones retain their freedom or die? Everything that happens to us amidst the situation that surrounds us still comes down to freedom of choice. Who is this Mike Pence, the Vice President of the United States of America? "I'm a Christian, a conservative, and a Republican in that order," Pence stated in his speech to the Republican National Convention in 2016. He pledged to work alongside Donald Trump "for the sake of the rule of law, and sanctity of life, for the sake of the second amendment, and also for the sake of other God-given liberties." These two men, Pence and Trump, were selected by God, whether or not we like it, to come into power leading the greatest nation on the face of the earth—Pence the experienced political stalwart, younger and more tolerable to mainstream Republicans than President Trump. But don't ever take for granted Trump, who is the tribulation president. What is confusing about what I was shown in my vision of the Nebuchadnezzar statue that turned upside down is whether the Trump/Pence situation will play out the same way as the baton was passed on to Belshazzar, the son of Nebuchadnezzar, who saw the writing on the wall. It was through Belshazzar that the prophecy of Isaiah was fulfilled with the destruction of Babylon. Will the baton similarly pass from the older Trump to the younger Pence?

What the Lord has shown me in vision is not always clear or easy to interpret, nor was it meant to be, but as He speaks things into my heart and mind, so do I write. No matter what, He always shows me the meaning eventually, even though it sometimes takes years. I often go back to Him and ask Him what it meant, and usually I have to wait for the answer, though sometimes He tells me right there and then, sometimes He doesn't. This is the reason why He is the Mystery within a mystery. I pass it on to you, and then it's up to you to decide if you agree with my interpretation and what you will do with the information.

Look at Mrs. Clinton's choice of a running mate—Tim Kane, a man whose is more than qualified, ivy- league educated, and governor of one of the most progressive states, with an impressive resume. Is it a coincidence that, both Kane and Pence, has Jesuit connections, and was both chosen for vice-president position on both sides of the aisle, being in line as the 45th potential president choices? No, it is not. What many fail to understand is that this is real, and I wish I could blast it from the mountain top for the whole world to hear. But I cannot because it was not meant to be, or people would be able to hear that message instead of sitting in front of the television listening to the same story and propaganda of feel-good prosperity religion. Jesus is coming, and many will be found wanting when they could have been saved if they only knew the truth. Yes, the essential truth! Is there a possibility that the vice president will sometime in the great tribulation become the president of the United States? I really don't know, but from what I'm seeing it may be so, for whatever reason. The stage is set for the greatest fulfillment of the Revelations, to personify the abomination of desolation which is foretold in Mathew 24:15. He will be in the position to give power to the beast of Revelation 13. If I'm correctly hearing what The Lord is telling me (never ever wanting to run before Him, but to always follow Him as a humble servant), Vice President Pence will be the one to fulfill Revelation 13, as he will be torn between doing the bidding of the pope and preserving the constitution of the United States. The impetus will be for church and state to once again remarry to re-institutionalize the blue laws, the national Sunday law that will be instated under the new world order through which the Jesuits hope to realize their most sacred ambition of controlling this republic.

What I must make clear is that, there is nothing wrong with being a Catholic if it's in ignorance we continue walking in the wilderness of confusion. But to whom much is given, much is required. When you learn the truth and some of the things that The Lord God has shown me, then you might have a change of heart, those who has chosen religion over the essential truth. Many of them will come to accept the essential truth in the millions because they are among Gods children, those with the pure in heart, for "blessed are the pure in heart for they shall see God." But the prophecy must be fulfilled and Vice President Pence will have no choice but to allow it to come to fruition, though he is as yet unaware of it. Vice President Pence's conscience will have him thinking that he will be doing the right thing, and in the process he will fulfill one of the greatest prophecies of Revelation 13, which every Christian who does not know God the Father and have a personal relationship with Him fears greatly.

It is through creeping compromise that everything will happen, and as I have stated before, what I was shown tells me that it will happen in record speed. I will show you where we are as a people who chose to forget, though it doesn't really matter because what is to be must be and will be, and this is the reason why I have been given the privilege of writing this book as the final warning. The secret behind the secret is that there is no escape from the time table of the Most High God. His prophetic time clock is precise. Is it a coincidence that both Donald Trump and Hillary Clinton chose running mates with a connection to the Jesuits? Or this is of Devine design. These men who call themselves the Society of Jesus Christ, these are some of the most dangerous men on the face of the earth, stronger than all of the secret societies put together. These are all true agents of Lucifer; to understand them requires knowledge of their history and what they are all about. These are men that will stop at nothing to accomplish their assigned mission, no matter how long it takes, as it is always the end result that is paramount. Men of the caliber of Pence and Kane must never be taken lightly, despite their calm demeanor. It is men who, under the greatest disguise but blind as to their true mission, have infiltrated the system and planted seeds that have taken root deeply in the fabric of America the greatest country on earth. Her original intention: Freedom of religion, where church and state are supposed to be separate and afar from each other where people can live in peace and not threatened with losing their lands and belonging and eventually their lives because of their beliefs.

America pledged under the constitution not to ever repeat the power and control of the catholic church in Europe in the dark – ages did with its citizens . It was inhumane, much darker that the deepest and darkest valley you can imagine, of which speak its own sadistic and dark language just by the name "the Dark Ages" The people in those days were been executed like nothing you've ever seen or heard of before. Some men and women pledge not to forget even though these Jesuits would hope we all forget. A time in the history of the world that people rather put behind them. Sad to say but history often repeats itself. These are men that must not be taken lightly. Still, you must have no fear, because God is with those who love Him and keep His commandments. Again this race will never be for the fast or the swift ,but to the man that endureth unto the end. You will be put to the test ,you must know what to look for and what sequence they will come in. The Lord God will never keep His children in the dark ,He will always send someone to remind us and be that candle in the dark.

Chapter 19

The Private Thoughts of The Forefathers of America: Outspokenness of Presidents in The Raw….. "The Jesuits"

WERE THESE MEN OUT OF THEIR MINDS?

The founding fathers of America knew the nature of the beast and understood the deadly disguise of the dragon. They understood that even the elect of God would be deceived. Here is what John Adams (president Adams) wrote to Thomas Jefferson (president Jefferson) in the spring of May 1816 about the "restoration" of the Society of Jesus: "I do not like the reappearance of the Jesuits…Shall we not have regular swarms of them here, in as many disguises as only a king of the Gipsies can assume, dressed as printers, publishers, writers and school masters? If ever there was a body of men who merited damnation on earth and in hell, it is this society of Loyola's. Nevertheless, we are compelled by our system of religious toleration to offer them an asylum." The Society of Jesus Christ was founded on obedience to the pope, which naturally raises questions about conflicting allegiances. John Adams had his suspicions, knowing the nature of the beast and what history has taught us, though many seem to have forgotten or have chosen to forget. Adams would continue "and then there's the whole catholic thing."

Indeed, Thomas Jefferson wrote two years earlier, "What could be invented to debase the ancient Christians, which Greeks, Romans, Hebrews, and Christians faction above all the Catholics, have not fraudulently imposed upon the public?" It was in 1821 that John Adams, the second president of the United States and one of the framers of our great constitution asked, "Can a free government possibly exist with the Roman Catholic religion?" Adams was a no nonsense critical thinker, as outspoken and pragmatic as they come. Only those who understand history and how it affects our spirituality will stand up for the truth in this moment in time. Revelation 13 is about to be fulfilled, and the apostle John was shown in a vision what will decide this very moment in time that I speak of: "And I stood upon the sand of the sea and saw a beast rise up out of the sea having seven heads and ten horns, and upon his horns ten crowns, and upon his head the name of blasphemy. And the beast which I saw was like unto a leopard and his feet were as the feet of a bear and his mouth as the mouth of a lion; and the dragon gave him his power, and his seat and great authority. And I saw one of his heads as it were wounded to death; and his deadly wound was healed; and all the world wondered after the beast. And they worship the dragon which gave power unto the beast; and they worship the beast, saying who is like unto the beast? Who is able to make war with him? And there was given unto him to continue forty and two months. And he opened his mouth in blasphemy against God, to blaspheme His name and His tabernacle and they that dwell in heaven.

And it was given unto him to make war with the saints, and to overcome them. And power was given him over all peoples and tongues and nations. And all that dwell upon the earth shall worship him whose name is not written in the book of life of the Lamb slain from the foundation of the world. If any man have an ear let him hear." It is this prophecy that we are on the brink of fulfilling. You need not take my word for it, as time will tell. The sad thing is that many will not believe, and it might be too late before they wake up from their slumber by design—the great deception of feel good religion and information /media overload designed to distract you into total submission to the beast that will rob you of your soul, though some of us will give it up freely. The United States of America is the great beacon of democracy and is now at risk of losing its integrity on the world stage because of the policies of President Trump and his vision of the world. But it is by no accident that we are where we are today. The stage has been set for the beginning of the end, and there is no turning back on the path that we are now on.

This is not like the Jonah story. This time, God will not withdraw His wrath if Nineveh repents. This is, unfortunately, the reality of our human existence. It is for the sake of His elect that what must happen will happen, though I can't tell you how it will play out over the next four years and the four more after that to the end of the great tribulation under this presidency. I don't really know the plans of The Lord God of The Most High. I can only write what is given to me. The same powers have moved all the men of significance that ended up on the wrong side of history. They may claim to have had no control over their actions, but it is because of their choices along the path of life's journey that they are compelled to fulfill their purpose. Each of us comes to earth for a different reason, some for good and some for evil, yet each of us has the freedom to choose our path through life. Mike Pence was raised in Indiana during the 1960s, in an Irish–Catholic, Democratic family, and once considered becoming a Catholic priest. Much has been made of the fact that Pence at one time described himself as an "Evangelical Catholic," but writing for the Indianapolis Monthly in 2013, Craig Furman reported that Pence has become reticent and discreet about the shift in his faith and would rather be regarded as an ordinary Christian. Though Pence distances himself from his Catholic roots, the secret behind the secret is that he continued to call himself a Catholic until the mid-1990s. Michelle Boorstein of the Washington Post noted that it was during this period when "white evangelicals and conservative Catholics in the United States started to realize that they had a lot more in common than their more denominationally tribal parents realized." For example, both Catholics and evangelical Christians have worked to protect "traditional" marriage and advocate for tightening abortion restrictions. Pence, a six-term congressman before becoming Vice President, is widely respected by Republicans, especially House Speaker Paul Ryan, who is often critical of Donald Trump's inflammatory rhetoric. Pence's support of Indiana's controversial religious freedom bill brought him national acclaim among conservative evangelical Christians who want to reverse the tide of same sex marriage in America, but the secret behind the secret is that it's too late. President Obama's role was to put in place all the pieces to open the door to the abomination of desolation, the beginning of the end. He did this as the 44th president of the United States of America. Bear in mind that the number 4 represents prophetic change throughout biblical history. What is to be must be God forbid.

Chapter 20

America The Mother Hen of The World & The End of The NRA.....

"America isn't it The Mother hen of The World?

On November 8, 2016, I wrote (in a political forecast I publish before the election) that Americans will, indeed, vote not with their conscience but with their hearts. They fell for Lucifer's deception, believing that foreigners are stealing jobs from them and their children. They forgot that America is the world's pregnant mother of freedom, always giving birth to a new idea that rocks the world and causes everyone around the globe to pay attention. They ignore the fact that many of the jobs held by immigrants American-born citizens deem downgrading. I had a few of those jobs after coming to America as a young lad before becoming a citizen of this great country. My children can identify with my experiences, as can the rest of us who came from somewhere else and found solace under the wings of this great mother hen whose chicks are of many colors, ethnicities, and religions.

A mother hen doesn't favor one hatchling over another. Her chicks are all her chicks, and she gives them all the same shelter and the same treatment. She scratches in the dirt so all may eat, and will fight off predators to protect each and every one of her babies, regardless of its color. It's the fittest of the fittest that survive, as nature has its own way of eliminating the weak. America is that mother hen of the world, and it has been her wings that sheltered so many fleeing persecution. America is the place of refuge God prepared for His children persecuted by the hundreds of thousands in Europe for their faith when the catholic church was more powerful than the state and kings and queens dared not defy it.

The sad news is that this time around America will become the persecutor of religious freedom. Who will believe this? I know it's hard to digest but wait and you will see for yourself.

This president, as well as this moment in time will embrace a different idea like nothing you've seen before, as I have warned you and will continue to warn you is the sleeping giant that you were once afraid of. Well he will be the one they chose / allowed to bring peace to the shores of America and the chaos that is about to ignite around the world from the catastrophe that lingers over our heads. It's not if it's going to happened, it's a matter of when.

In the spring of 2016 I heard one commentator on the radio, on 90.5 FM say that "it is not candidate Donald Trump with his unfiltered speech, crude manners, and tendency to bend the truth that scares him". What he says frightens him is how far the American people are willing to go down the path of no return. There is no more reverence for life. It is so sad that we are entertained by the destruction of others. Reality shows get bolder and more provocative and movies get more violent. Sexually explicit scenes and profanity abound on prime time television, when your children or grandchildren may be watching. And we can't seem to get enough of this entertainment, of this creeping compromise that will take us deeper into the cesspool of today's reality. You will see why this is imminent and how it will manifest itself in the presidency of Donald Trump, who continues to use the tactics that tore apart the Republican establishment and are polarizing the population. He will speak the language of the day and tell you exactly what you want to hear. Even people who can't stomach his rhetoric personally will vote for him by the millions because he promised them what they need, want, and believe they deserve.

It is not by the hands of a woman, Hillary Clinton, or a Jew, Bernie Sanders, that this great country will tumble into the hands of the Jesuits, but by a demagogue who knows that America is the envy of the world. Remember, it's not the actuality that is most dangerous but rather the intention behind the actuality.

Chapter 21

Trading Morality for Power and Greed

"Trading Morality for Power and Greed...... Was This Written In The Books of Life?

America will trade her morality for power and greed, which is to say that the conservative movement of the Republican Party is a thing of the past. Enjoy with Godly fear the last moment of the good times and prepare for the worst. And The NRA will become a thing of the past when President Trump orders the confiscation of guns, convincing you to give away your liberty in exchange for security, which will only serve to help usher in the New World Order. You might smile at this one, but wait and you'll see.

From the moment that Trump announced his run for the presidency, I told anyone who would listen that he would be the next president, just as I predicted Bill Clinton ultimate election victory the very day he announced his candidacy, and also Barrack Obama's even in his darkest moment with Reverend Jeremiah. And those messages from the Lord were never as clear as what I've now been shown. I put my conviction about a Trump presidency out to the world on Facebook in February of 2016, but have been on talk radio speaking of this premonition from 2015, just to show that what was given to me is not of my own understanding but of a higher order, from the ONE who called me to come up into His holy Mountain 24 years ago.

"We have to be careful of what we do, or how we treat others in these last moments of earth's history, and must be aware that we have been tested in every way, and every moment of the day. Whatever you do is going to come back to you and if it doesn't come back that simple means that you haven't made it….to the Promised Land! And will be left out or found wanting" It is with this narrative that Donald Trump won the women's vote over Hillary Clinton, who was positioned to become the first woman U.S. president, but the secret behind the secret is that prophecy must be fulfilled. President Donald Trump will govern for the seven years of the tribulation period, and you will see the true nature of the beast.

Deep in many of your hearts, you know he is speaking your language, though most lack the guts to acknowledge it. The racism that we suppressed for years will finally jump out along with all of our other prejudices. In the 2016 election, which could be America's last election,(considering that this presidency will take us to the end, to a president Trump /Pence) there will be no middle ground. Everyone must take a side, whether they voted or not, and will continue to do so because there still is no middle ground as we move on into a darker and graver reality of the end of the world as we know it.

Chapter 22

The Time of Jacob's Trouble Is upon Us!

"HOW MANY OF US WILL BE ABLE TO STAND.......IN THIS TIME?"

………….May God Be With You All……………

The black hole of history is repeating itself in front of our very eyes, and the sad thing is that there is nothing any of us can do to stop the great hemorrhaging of morality around the world. Can't you see what is really going on that shows this to be the beginning of sorrow, which is called the time of Jacob's trouble? In the time of Jacob's trouble, man will mock God (the force and power behind homosexuality is a great example as the churches cave in to such idea of acceptance ,even though they know it's not of God) But will turn their heads as well as their consciences to appease the masses. The heart of men will wax cold in this time as we get further and further from the truth from the essential truth . Is it man's desire that must be up-held or Gods way for a better tomorrow that is most important? just like in the days of Sodom and Gomorrah and make fun of the prophecies while everything ungodly becomes the norm, just as in in the days of Noah when man tuned out the word of God. Sexual immorality is center stage in America and there is chaos in the White House which will get worse faster than any one can imagine, just as I have seen in the vision of the end. You might think it's a joke, but the time of Jacob's trouble is upon us, and most of us are still sleeping and will be found sleeping in the time when we should have extra oil in our lamps.

The final days of God's mercy are about to expire. The morality of America has caved in, our elected officials ridicule each other, and the entire world is watching as the birthplace of modern democracy succumbs to demagoguery. Many great patriotic Americans will try to keep the flag of democracy flying, but pretty soon their arms will get tired, and they will find themselves having to choose, as all who live on the face of the earth will have to do— rich and poor, great and small, free and shackled alike. I'm sorry to tell you the truth that is staring you in the face. I'm sorry to be the doomsday prophet, but I must deliver what was given to me, because it's not about me but about The One who has sent me. Though many will take to the street in civil disobedience and the thousands that march will become hundreds of thousands as the word spreads like wildfire, I'm sorry to say it will not change anything other than to perhaps slow things down. Nothing will change the prophetic time clock of The Most High. Man's time is over. This is now God's time and what is to be must be!

The beginning of the end is here. The Lord God of The Most High showed me these words written on the walls of heaven: "It Is done!!" The demonstrations in the streets of America, and even around the world, against President Trump's executive orders will backfire because they are not directed at the GOP establishment but against the president himself, and he has a major role to play in what is to unfold. He will wield dictatorial power never before seen in America, and the media will soon be a thing of the past, censored by popular demand as the conscience of America falls into the pits of no return as we are urged and manipulated to turn on each other. Racism will be preached from a politico-religious platform and in social media, soon creeping into the very fabric of our consciousness.

Though the head of the stream is polluted, by design it will be the powerless that will pay the price. Is it fair and just that we lock up our youths for emulating the disrespect they see in their elders when it is the head of the stream that is contaminated, and not the brooks that carry the tributaries or run-off? The name calling and juvenile behavior of the politicians is deplorable. The deplorable language and behavior our children witness every day create a tangled web of a greater deception that we will never be able to untangle or escape with the noose around our children's neck.

Nothing that is going on in America's political arena or on the world stage is a coincidence. Everything is going exactly the way The Most High God planned it. It is by Divine design that events are unfolding, so rapidly and surreally that many are as yet blind to the truth. Immorality theology is taking over the world, and if you're not a critical thinker you'll never know the truth. The great secret behind the wildest secret is that Lucifer is an illusionist, promising things that he cannot deliver, and this is how he got caught up in God's business that he had no business in and now is facing eternal damnation. For thousands upon thousands of years, he has been selling something his delusionary mind conjured up, deceiving the world since the beginning of time. But in the end, he will get his just reward when the Lord God of The Most High comes to reclaim his own.

The immorality that is rampant in society today fulfills the prophecy of 2nd Timothy 3: "But know this, that in the last days, perilous times will come. For men will be lovers of themselves, lovers of money, boasters, proud, blasphemers, disobedient to parents, unthankful, unholy, unloving and unforgiving. Slanderers without self- control, brutal, despisers of good traitors headstrong, haughty, lovers of pleasures rather than lover of God; having a form of Godliness, but denying the truth thereof."

For every reason, there is a greater meaning or reason behind it. It is said that absolute power corrupts absolutely, and what the world is about to see come to fruition under President Trump is absolute power. And don't comfort yourself by thinking, "This too shall pass," because it will not pass this time. This time is the last time around, and fasting and prayer will not hold back the winds of change that will be upon us. Everything that is done from this day onward will only get worse as time fades away into the unknown between time and space, never to return. Solomon said that nothing is new under the sun, but what is about to come has never been seen before on the face of the earth. It is said of this time, in Matthew 24:11, "And many false prophets will arise and lead many astray." In these days that are about to come upon us, wickedness will multiply and the hearts of men will grow cold. It is within this time that false doctrines will multiply, and love will have no longer have a place in the hearts of men.

We are living in the time when people are trampling the blood of Jesus Christ under their feet, prostituting the word of God for a profit selling feel-good religion cloaked in the deception of prosperity. You'll wake up one morning in the middle of the great tribulation and can't believe that it's really here, and may find that it is eternally too late for your soul's salvation. We are all going to wake up to the screams of people unable to believe or comprehend what they are seeing before their very eyes. It will be an unbelievably sad day for the millions upon millions of people who wait for the very last moment in time to get their house in order. Only those who are prepared for this great and most feared day that is almost upon us will escape such an atrocity. The five wise virgins that have extra oil in their lamps will be the only ones able to climb these mountains of the seven years of tribulation and survive somewhere far from the world's major population centers.

If you're not making preparation now to get out of these cities and go underground before the abomination of desolation begins, then you will be among those who will find themselves crying over spilled milk, realizing that they have waited too long, not understanding that humanity's time has run out. It's now God's time. If we do not line ourselves up to trim our lamps to travel through the nights while there is time (but not in the winter or on His holy Sabbath day), then it will be too late. You will be among those who will be carried off to the camps that have already been built in preparation for this very moment in time. These FEMA camps will be filled to capacity, and many will be saying they cannot do this to us as Americans.

But you would know otherwise if you had read the scriptures of Daniel and the revelation showing that this must come to pass before the coming of The Lord. This is why He said, "Be wise in knowing thee; I sent you as sheep among wolves. Be as wise as a serpent and harmless as a dove." Who do you think will fill up these camps? Cows and goats and dogs and cats? The children of God are not exempt from such persecution. Indeed, you must count it a blessing to be persecuted for The Lord God of The Most High, who himself was crucified. Count it a blessing, and have no fear because God will be with those who are ready for this journey. Many will think that they are ready, but sad to say it is easier said than done. Many who have enjoyed a life of luxury on earth will have a hard time not looking back when this time comes. You might think you can do it, but let me warn you, if it's not out of love for The Most High God and love only, you won't be able to do it. Many of you will change your mind when you realize that you have to leave your nice comfortable bed and your warm hot showers and make do with a cold misty morning dip in river water. When you think of giving up your luxurious car or that big SUV that shows the neighbors your buying power and status (something most of us in the Western world are very much guilty of) and picture yourself climbing mountains and running through ditches, it won't be easy to make the journey.

When you think of the delicious meals you can cook in minutes, or the refrigerator full of food that stands between you and hunger, will you be willing to walk away into the wind and caves of uncertainty, it's sad to say, but you will surely think twice. Only those who serve Him out of love and only love, will be able to deal with such atrocity or be able to make such sacrifice. If it's not love you will look back, just like Lot's wife. The great secret behind the secret is that Lucifer is selling countless millions this wicked deceptive lie, searching for the ally that he has long sought to aid him in fighting against the Most High. But he has not found such an ally yet, and never will because God is God and God Alone. You will find that as you look around and contemplate all of the above of Jacobs trouble you'll realize that its easier said than done. How many of us will really choose the road less traveled and will be able to deal with the up-hill battle that lies ahead instead of the lily-white fields that these preachers are brainwashing you about, with their feel-good religion. If it was meant to be that easy Christ wouldn't have to come to die. If it was that easy He would have never said "If it was possible even the very elect of God would have been lost" If it was possible. Don't let them lie to you my dear friends ,my brothers and sisters who you all know who you are, again please don't let them lie to you about this great deceptive trap that lies ahead and is waiting to devour all those who can be devoured. Get ready to run and prepare to travel light. The Lord said in this moment in time if you find yourself on the roof of your house don't go inside to fetch extra clothing run as you are!! And pray that you're not pregnant if you're a woman and pray also that it's not in the winter Times or on the Sabbath day where you have to go and gas up your car or truck for the journey.

Remembered God is not mocked ……He will do exactly what He said He will Do . Because He does what He means and means what He said".

Chapter 23

The Chosen Ones: Will Abraham's Seed Matter In The End?

The Chosen One: Will Abraham's Seed Matter in the End?

The breath and life of humanity's freedom is on the brink of destruction in America and around the world because so many are driven by greed, ego, hate, and power. Very few abide by truth and righteousness and uncorrupted love. The great news is that God's people are still living on earth, though few and far between, and you'll still find them when it matters most. Still, it was Abraham that was chosen by God to fulfill His purpose. It was Abraham who was ordained to usher in the greatest event on the face of the earth since the creation of man, and it was through him that the seed would be planted to bring in The Messiah. That seed would be fulfilled in Jacob, otherwise known as Israel, who would sire Judah, the fourth son of the blessed union ordained by God Himself. Although Rachael was Jacob's pride and joy, Leah was God's chosen. The secret behind the secret is that no man can decide for God, because He is God and God Alone The Mystery within a mystery. The birth of The Lord God of The Most High, Yashua the Christ, was planted in Abraham's seed and made manifest in Judah. Through Him the highest order known to man was established on the face of the earth, put into place for this very moment in time. It is no mistake that we are who we are, and those that emulate

His love and mercy are of the highest order on earth, and are different from the rest of the world for a reason.

The order of Melchizedek was the highest order ever known on earth until The Son of The Most High God, Jesus Christ, came to save us from our sins and many of us from ourselves. He came to deliver us from the spiritual Egypt's around the world, whose intention is to hold us in captivity, bringing the children of God under subjugation by Satan's greatest deceptions. But Christ came and set the captives free. Now it's up to you and me to set ourselves free through the choices we make from this day onward in the great tribulation years that are about to come upon us.

Melchizedek was the mystery man. He was the king of Salem and priest of The Most High, who lived in righteousness on earth before God called Abraham. These are men who kept the laws of God always in their hearts, long before The Most High gave the laws in physical form to Moses on Mount Sinai. It is for this very reason that I was sent to you and why I was given these few words of wisdom to pass on to you for you to pass on to your loved ones. Know that The Merciful and Compassionate God who is also a God of vengeance, whose love and mercy endure forever, will always give mortal man ample time to get it right. After that, it's sudden destruction.

As always, blood has to be shed to set God's children free, just as it was shed to free Israel from slavery in America and around the world—brothers killing brothers over differences in philosophy and belief. This was no accident, but rather what had to happen. We must understand that for every action there is an equal reaction, whether or not we embrace it. Destiny is a pattern that will eventually become your reality, as nature holds every one of us accountable for our deeds, and we often forget that it doesn't forget. God gives every one of us our just reward, and we Israelites, God's chosen, get ours for our disobedience against Him. But woe to the ones who subject us to atrocities for they, too, will be held accountable for their sins. America was chosen, handpicked by God The Most High as a place of refuge where all people from around the world could escape the religious persecution that was prevalent in Europe at the time, when the Catholic church controlled governments and was persecuting the innocents by the millions. America has become the land of freedom where men, women, and children from all over the earth and every walk of life come for religious freedom, but eventually become persecutors themselves.

As it is written in Revelation 13:11 – 14: "And I beheld another beast coming up out of the earth and he has two horns like a lamb, and he speaks like a dragon; and he exercised all the powers of the first beast before him, and caused the earth and them that dwell therein to worship the first beast, whose deadly wound was healed. And he doeth great wonders, so that he makes fire come down from heaven on the earth in the sight of man, and deceived them that dwell on the earth by the means of those miracles which he had power to do in the sight of the beast, saying to them that dwell on the earth that they should make an image to the beast which had the wound by a sword and did live."

The only beast of all the beasts that come out of the earth that represents America. She is the lamb-like beast, and what is to be must be. Slavery was no mistake, from the arrival of the first African in Virginia in 1619.

Those who were affected by the great persecution of the Catholic church and the middle passage understand this very well, though some choose to forget. If you have never been oppressed or persecuted, you will never understand this kind of narrative, but pretty soon you'll know because no man will be able to escape what is to come. The only escape is to be one with The Lord God of The Most High, Yashua The Christ Himself. America's civil war was the worst bloodbath ever seen on her soil, started on April 12, 1861 one hundred and fifty five years ago, which wasn't a long time, where the blood of our countrymen was shed to water the tree of liberty that so many have taken for granted. To forget would be the greatest sin and a total dishonor to this great country. The secret behind the secret is that we would rather believe a lie than embrace the truth, even when it's right in front of you. We are now at the end of the world as we know it, though many will not believe it because everything still looks normal. But those who choose to fly on the wings of ignorance will never reach the eternal shore because they don't take the time to seek the wisdom and understanding that come only from the Lord. This is why so many will lose, because once the great tribulation begins and they realize that it is here it may be too late. You may find yourself begging for mercy when the door of probation has already been closed. As in Thessalonian 5:3, "For when they shall say there is peace and safety, then there is sudden destruction, as travail upon a woman with child and they shall not escape." The truth of the matter is that I can only show you what the Lord God of the Most High has shown me. I was not sent to convert you or to condemn you, but I cannot sugar coat these few last words that were given to me by The Most High God Himself.

This is no time for band aids or feel-good religion. What I will show you in the Black Books of Moses may be the very last warning directly from The One who has sent me. The Lord God of The Most High is the only One who can choose who will come. Let me warn you that what you are about to see will not sit well with many, but

I did not call myself. I am only a humble servant sent to you in this saddest time in the history of the world, though the preachers and teachers and politicians will tell you different while the news media regurgitate what they say and put their spin on it to sway you in the greatest deception that is about to come upon the earth. And many of us will be deceived, God help us!

Affliction marks the road of prophecy, and we cannot get away from it. There is only one way around it, which I will show you as you journey with me through these Black Books of Moses. The key to the kingdom of heaven is hidden in the mystery of the parables, and only a few will find it. There will be much abuse and mockery and many false prophets whose prophecies will have nothing to do with your soul's salvation. It's going to be a great deception like nothing you have seen before. There will be many people who believe that they will be among the children of The Most High God when self-preservation and earthly treasures and wealth are their greatest concerns. Many of these feel-good religion preachers and false prophets will have to give an account for the greatest deception that will come upon man, and it is they who set the stage for the great tribulation.

We are at the point of no return. It was a beautiful world before we came and destroyed it, but now we must face the consequences of our destructive actions against God and man. The crime we chose to commit against The Most High God, whose love is still more powerful than His anger and is still in the business of saving us from our sins, is irreversible. How long will He keep calling us to come and find Him while there is time? How long will He wait upon us as God and God Alone? So many of us won't wake up in time. You might call me a doomsday prophet, but I wasn't sent to mince words about the great atrocity that is about to come upon mankind. And though His love and mercies toward us will never change, we humans have taken advantage of His love through which He gave us His only Begotten Son who died that we might live: "For God so love the world that He gave His only begotten son that whosoever believeth on Him should not perish but have everlasting life" (John 3:16). The greatest and most dangerous time in the history of the world is upon us, and we are too blind to see it. The things that I've been made privy to by The Lord God Himself are not anything that you really want to hear, but I must tell you anyway, because The Lord gave me, as His humble servant, the duty to share it with you. And you will have the privilege of making the greatest decision of your entire life.

Chapter 24

My Dream of The Writing on the Walls of Heaven

THE GREAT MYSTERIOUS CHECK-MARK OF DOOM - BY THE UNSEEN HANDS OF GOD

"IS ISRAEL IN GREAT DANGER!! – *LIKE NOTHING WE HAVE SEEN BEFORE? …...*"

Wake up Israel! Wake Up!!!

Wake up Israel, and make your path straight, Wake up!! Danger is on your door steps lurking in the dark in broad daylight, like a hungry lion seeking whom he may devour, and I must warn you, like nothing you've seen before is coming upon you. I wish I could tell you in details of what it is but that was not privy to me at this moment as I write. What I know for sure is that you are in great danger. My heart cries for you because I don't know what to do. This sad premonition came twice in one night. It all started after retiring for the night I lay my head down to sleep and in less than half an hour The Lord God of The Most High showed this vision to me. I was shown in a prophetic dream (that may be mixed with a vision) the greatest disaster that is to come upon us and what saddens my heart is that I don't know what it means. I saw writing on the walls of heaven as if this is the time of the end of the world, similar to the time of the end of Babylon in the Nebuchadnezzar dream. The writing on the walls of heaven went from east to west and one of the letters was written in blood. It was the letter "I" that was written in blood. The Spirit of The Lord tells me that the "I" represents Israel, and that Israel must be prepared for whatever tragedy will come upon them during the tribulation time or before such, that will be upon us sooner than we think.

I hate to be the doomsday prophet, but I must tell you what I saw, and what is almost upon us and I must say it's not pretty. I really hate to be the carrier of bad news and I really wish it was different but I have no control over what The Lord shows me. All I am is just a messenger sent with a message of which you might not even believe much less to accept. It will be totally up to you to embrace or dismiss it. In a prophetic dream that came to me in the fall of 2016 just like the vision I had in the same time period last year November in the fall of 2015, in this very same time, when I was privy to the coming of The Lord God of The Most High of heaven and earth, that you must see in "we all have been deceive": when the sun gave way to the moon and the moon gave way to the star; and what happened next is unbelievable of what I saw (you will see this vision in the volume 2 of these chronicles). It was in the same time period of the latter I saw writing on the walls of heaven.

I was taken in The Spirit to this unknown location, of which I was beckon to look up as I was looking in the sky the heavens became dark and gray as if an omen of doom is lurking over the entire world. I was not standing on the ground it seems and where I was I cannot tell you because I don't know. As I watched the sky change to a cloud of doom I had no clue what to expect, then out of nowhere flash across the sky in the darkness of the clouds where words that I had no clue of what it meant or what it represents. Is this the mysterious hand of Almighty God writing on the walls of heaven? As I gazed into the bitter invidious sky

what I saw will break a grown man's heart, no matter how strong of a warrior he is. This is the hand of God writing on the walls of heaven. It came in this mysterious puzzle in the letters of "I – C- W- S -Y – Z" and I was unsure of what it is or could possible means and am still un-sure of it all, but I am almost sure that this is what I saw, because everything happened so fast. I was awakened by such mystical encounter in this troublesome dream and I woke up in Godly fear. I asked The Lord what could this means and there was no answer. I lay my head down again after I asked The Lord God who reveals every secret of the heart "what was the writing, and what could it possible means?" And low and behold the very same dream or vision reoccur and it scared me greatly. I couldn't believe that I was seeing the very same vision playing out on the walls of heaven. And it bothers me deeply. What made it really; really mysterious is that one of the letters the very first letter standing in the Far East (as it appears in the heavens) was the letter "I", there was something dark and uncannily striking and scary attached to its lay-out. As I looked in astonishment I realized it was written in blood. It was big letters bold enough for the world to see it, yet no one saw it. I suppose for whatever reason God has in His time –clock of mystery decided somehow to let me have a glimpse of tomorrow. I was then taken by the spirit into another place that looks like the gates of hell, yes the Door-way to hell.

Chapter 25

…The Door Way To Hell…

" THE DOOR-WAY TO HELL?"

…This is a total different experience ever to be shown to me. I was in a place without any physical body just my soul peeping through the gates of hell it seems. A place where night and day have no say, a place where your emotion has no boundaries or your heart a place to lay its heavy burden. There's no one to talk to. As I looked on in the deepest of fear, realizing that I'm in the valley of the shadow of death, I pray and hope that it's really a dream and I'll be able to wake up from it. As I stood there looking in, something caught my eyes. I saw a round table sitting in the middle of no-where in the center of a room. On the table is a stock of cards. Out of the midst of the darkness mixed in loneliness, I heard the sadness of the human soul, which is in torment and hoping that they can go home someday after their life sentence is over, not knowing that it will never be over. I looked around in agony and pray to my Father that this is really a dream, hoping that what I'm seeing and feeling is temporary, and not forever. Even though my many sins is equivalent to such reward in a place like this ; because it is written "the wages of sin is death, but the gift of God is eternal life through Jesus Christ our Lord" Roman 6;23

The Lord God has been more merciful to me undeserving though I be. You are praying and hoping you might be able to wake up from this nightmare of doom, but it's too late. It's like hemorrhaging of the soul with no one to call upon for help. You're on your own in this state of mind forever and a day. I hear a baby crying in the distance a faint and wicked cry, the saddest of cry that will make any grown man weep much less a mother's heart hearing the grip of death around a baby's neck and you cannot help it. On top of it all I heard laughter, and more laughter voices coming from a place of insanity anchored in madness, mixed with sadness from the place of no return. This is the moment you wish that you were never born. You really, really wish you never was, when the cry of the infant child in piercing misery attached to your ear-drums that sounded like subdued pain mixed in sorrow, attached to the laughter of madness in the dungeon of un- forgiveness, on the throne of a hopeless soul sits the king of regrets. Crowns upon crowns of regrets, and it is much too late to negotiates another contract on the journey of life. We only get one shot at this, knowing that there's no repentance after the grave. Here comes the reality of the end of a hopeless soul, who has spent his or her life- time in a bed of sorrow, drunken with the wine of self-pity and unhappiness. Some with good intention but never get around to pull it together, but who's to be blame? It is just now you realize that all along you were dining with the harlot of the world, dressed in scarlet wearing the crown of deception sipping on the wine of immorality while pretending to be sublime. To the Door-way or Gate-Way of Hell, your soul is been dangled….. As I hovered in the spirit looking down on the table in the middle of heaven and hell the only thing that was on that table and place of no return was a deck of cards. As I was pulled closer to it in the spirit, there I could see events after events going in speed that I could not keep up with. I watched in Godly fear as the past flew by and the future of man disappears. My mind and heart was unable to be in peace much less in one accord, because in the midst of it all I still hear the piercing cry of the baby crying, and people laughing as the pages of history of yesteryears mixed with what is to come is on the table passing right in front of my very eyes, with unbelievable events after events. I wonder what could this means or what does this have to do with Israel and the blood in the sky? What is it The Lord God of The Most High is showing me and I'm not getting it? Because this is much deeper than what I'm seeing I said to myself, as I watched in agony. I wonder how many men and women will ever be able to make it out of this place I asked myself? You wouldn't wish this on your worst enemy. A place where the soul is subdued in a hellish reality is the saddest of life's unknown actuality where the soul cannot die. If this is not hell and is just the door-way to the place of no return, there's no words to fathom the agony of sin, within a sin-sick soul who have waited much too long to get off the train of no return on the tracks running along the highway to hell. The Gate-way of hell there's no story to tell reason is how many ever get out? *Not One!.* What on Gods earth could this possibly mean?

Am I been privy to the abomination of desolation? That is to come and is almost upon us? Could this letter "I" I saw written in blood also represent Israel to be annihilated by some great deception? Embracing the pope of Rome knowing that their most coveted and greatest ambition is to hold on to the temple mount to secure the seat of the antichrist? This I cannot take for granted, even though men in this time think that The Lord God of The Most High does not speak to mortal man anymore; as I have seen in dreams and visions and the great illusion mixed in deception. Is it really true that The Most High does not speak to mortal man anymore? The answer is yours to keep, but I must tell you that it is not true. He still have His chosen children here on earth that He chooses to speak to, when He is ready in His own time. You'll be surprised to know who they are , some of them you wouldn't be mindful of, but that's how The Most High works who is God and God Alone. You'll be surprised some of the things He chooses to shows His chosen ones. Just as He has been speaking to me for years now, and many others like myself. I must tell you that the gate-way to hell is real and sad and lonely.

This ain't no scare tactics , reason is I was not sent to convert you or to condemn you …..The Lord god of The Most High after leaving heaven and finding myself back on earth , I was told to only tell you. And was specifically sent to the house of the minorities.

A Glimpse of The Book Of Life- A Dear Sister's Vision

Were the names written in this book, contain the name of the 144,000 that is here on earth, right now living in this very moment in time ? Is the trillion dollar question that baffles my mind.

I met a dear sister a couple of years ago in the south, whom I was very intrigued by and am blessed to have met. She is without a doubt one of God's anointed, I met her on her death bed in Florida. Though she was ill, she was the one who was doing the encouraging, and I was very moved by that. She also is privy to similar prophetic dreams and visions, of which today, she is a stalwart for the Lord, not in the gift of gab but in action.

Over the years we shared the dreams and visions that we had been privy to trying to understand the things we're seeing. When she told me of the angel that appears to her in a dream, who picked up a huge, dusty brown book from out of the ground, I realize that she has been privy to one of the great secrets of God, because in this book, were the names of God's anointed written. Or was it the 144,000 that will live through the great tribulation that she has been privy to?

As she was looking, trying to get a close glimpse of the mystery of heaven, she really wondered if her name was written there. I could only tell her what she already knows I assumed, that this great phenomena, only a few are privy to such mysterious privileges.

I told her maybe it's a sign of the beginning of the end, when the sealing of God's children is on the horizon. Still we cannot get complacent in this time, when the work of God is most prevalent. Though the true gospel (the old time religion) today seem like an endangered species been compromised by prosperity religion, with the intention to debunk the essential truth. Still we must keep the candle of truth burning making sure we have extra oil in our lamps. I realize that The Most High, has sent His holy angel to come and speak to her specifically, as a sign of His eminent appearance that many on earth will not be ready for, How blessed she is to have such an encounter, I was thinking of my very own children, my brothers who some of them are still playing with fire, my sisters as well as the rest of the family, if their names will be there, as she told me in great detail what she saw.

This great book was shown to her for a specific reason, and also for a specific time. I wonder what this could mean.

She gave me a little snip of its content as she explained the mysterious detail of the book, " I paused to think of the right words to say, but realized that it is one of the mysteries within a mystery that she has been privy to. "I was looking for my name Mutti!" she said ,with a seriousness in her voice ; and I wish I had the answer to such premonition. I could only encourage her as she had often encouraged me, telling her that it's very possible that her name will be written there, but only if we are faithful unto the end.

I had assumed it was the book of life, as she had explained it in much detail and with great concern, mostly for our loved ones. I said this to say, we must never in this life, ever take anything for granted, because The Lord God said "Only those that are faithful unto the end shall be saved. "Matthew 24:13. The sealing of the saints of God is going on right now as we speak. Do you think it's by coincidence, you are reading this book?

Only a heart that is willing to do the work of The Lord gets such premonition

knowing that we are perfectly flawed and are so undeserving of his wonderful love. I considered this to be a huge breakthrough in this time when only a few are hearing and seeing some of the mysteries of God. The ones He chose to reveal Himself unto are more than privileged but are favoured . You'll see some of her writings in a book entitled, "Thoughts from My Heart" By Kay Grant-Lawrence. The one that has snips of what I have just mentioned, I assumed entitled, "Seeking That Which I have Lost". Look for her books of visions and dreams, intertwined in poetic language, about her own experience while being on her dying bed. Again the question is, could this be the names of those who will go through the great tribulation that is right on our doorstep?. (A Must Read)

Chapter 26

Israel in Great Danger!! Like Nothing We've Seen Before

The biggest question is what could this writing on the walls of heaven means? And why there is the letter …… "I"……. written in blood in the sky? Can someone tell me why I'm seeing these things? Again what make it significant is that it was in the East that I saw the letters on the walls of heaven and it was only one of the letters in blood. Will Israel be under attack in the very near future? As The Lord God had shown me in vision that things that is about to come upon us is going to happened in rapid speed. Are we here on earth in the very moment of the night as in the days of Daniel's prophecy making a 360 degree turn back to the beginning of the end to commemorate the very end of the beginning of time? When the very night the Babylonians saw the writing on the walls of Babylon the hands of The Lord God of The Most High wrote what was written, to fulfill the prophecy of Isaiah who have foretold of his reign 140 years before the actuality and that very night came the destruction of Babylon. It was this moment that would commemorate the 70 years prophecy of the Jews been in captivity because of our disobedience against The Lord God of The Most High, as His chosen children here on earth. It was also in this very moment in time The Most High put into motion the 70 week prophecy for the messiah death and resurrection. Revealing the sequence of events that would have taken place before his return of which we are living on the very edge of this moment in time, which can be anytime now?

As in the end of the destruction of Babylon, (the very head of gold) on the Nebuchadnezzar image seen in his vision, so will it be in this moment as it is to come. It was this very dream given to Nebuchadnezzar that would have establish the prophetic blueprint of the world, Interpreted by Daniel in one of the greatest prophetic precision ever in the greater prophets of old. Isn't the writing on the walls of Babylon in the days of Nebuchadnezzar's son Belshazzar very, very significant and important for us in this time? The truth of the matter is that I'm puzzled, not knowing what to think or what this could possibly means. What I know for sure is that, I've been privy to a glimpse of Gods prophetic time table. Some of the very things that seems to have taken place in the beginning of time; to usher in the very birth of The Messiah, Yashua The Christ, when the hand writing of God came on the walls of Babylon to bring the prophecy of His immaculate Conception or birth one day closer, of which today is history and we now look for His great and mighty return. I believe that I am now shown the very beginning of the end of Time. I know it's hard to believe that I was shown these things, and I can understand why, because even I am amazed that The Lord God of The Most High would showed me things like these. A man who is perfectly flawed, and undeserving of such love, mixed with spiritual and mysterious encounters, but again can a man judge God? I did not call myself He was The ONE who has chosen me for reason I don't know. So I understand that you are scratching your heads wondering If you should believe. The truth of the matter is that it's up to you my dear friends, and foe because in the very same arena of life buried the swords under the benches of death to kill the messengers of God, and today will to be used in the same way as before, if so, so be it because I know that I am not exempt from such atrocity. Jesus Christ Himself and all the prophets before Him, and His messengers after Him, was not exempt, so who am I? But not before I deliver what I was sent to do if that day should come before the great return. After I have revealed to you some of the things that The Lord God of The Most High has made me privy to then what will be will be.

I Was Shown Both The Statue of Nebuchadnezzar & The Writing on The Walls

Just as God appointed Nebuchadnezzar to see the great mystery of the future of which he had no clue of what he was privy to. Still he was the one appointed to oversee the very first kingdoms of the four great kingdoms of which he was the greatest of them all,(the head of gold) It is this prophetic dream that would determine and put in place the blue-print of the future of the world as we know it. As men stand in awe and watch the prophecy of Daniel unfold today, they still wonder about this great mystery those who fail to believe. The secret behind the secret is that "nothing is new under the sun"- book of Ecclesiastes 1:9 (Solomon the wisest of all men says these words) What Daniel was shown has comes to life in a deeper sense and meaning, as he was shown the very same statue of the one Nebuchadnezzar saw, but what he got, was much greater than what Nebuchadnezzar have seen. He was given the interpretation thereof, of this great mystery that some men would only see as a dream, but Nebuchadnezzar knew better. Those who are privy to Gods prophetic time –clock knows it when they see it. Something none of us can describe. Daniel saw how each of these kingdoms would replace each other in succession, ending with the fourth kingdom, Rome who is still alive and well sleeping in the trenches of obscurity, hoping that you and I will forget. A-waiting the day of the great revenge of the Vatican is eminent. **It's Only**

Now I Started to Understand the Mysterious puzzle: All of this must come to fruition before the great and final day of The Lord God. Everything as in every kingdom or earthly powers must come to an end, and must be replaced by something greater. This time it will be replaced by the Kingdom of God and not the 3rd temple they will attempt to build in isreal. It is Donald Trump or his regime who will take the fourth kingdom that is scattered as in iron and clay, (which means there will never be another world power, until the baton is passed to the beast) to the very end of the world to fulfill Revelation 13, just as it is written in the prophecy.

It will be nothing strange to us who knows God and understand what is happening prophetically as the very same statue shown to me by The Lord God of The Most High comes to a screeching halt. It is now I understood that what I was shown is much deeper and important than I myself could ever believe. I am given the blueprint of the final moment of time. God help us! Isn't it amazing how I was shown the Nebuchadnezzar statue comes to a screeching halt and (4) four years after was shown the writing on the walls of heaven? What you and I must realize is that Babylon fell to the Medians and Persians —Cyrus The Great's name was mentioned in the Torah hundreds of years before he was even born, that he would be the one to deliver Israel from bondage. It happened precisely as it was written. It's going to be totally up to you, to decide your own destiny if there is still time. As it was prophesy after the writing comes on the walls, today I saw writings on the walls of heaven which signify something much, much sinister and deeper than any of us could ever imagine.[I will show you what The Lord God of The Most High will show me in these Revelations, in volume 2. of the chronicles]! It is only now when I put all the dreams and visions together on paper it started making sense to me. All along God was showing me something, much deeper than

I thought it could be, creating a different picture much, much more scarier than I could ever imagine. It is now I realized that I am given one of the greatest assignment given to modern man by The Lord God of The Most High, after you receive this weather or not you believe it, will be totally up to you, but my work will be done once it's been delivered. It was my biggest fair (dragging my feet on Gods prophetic time-clock the little piece of the puzzle that was given to me) if I had continued to be lackadaisical in creating my own spiritual demise but I had asked for forgiveness and The Lord has given me this second chance. I pray it won't be in vain after you see all of what was given to me, to give to you in these 4 chronicles.

Chapter 27

The Church Painted in Black – The Luke-warmness of God's People

The children of Abraham have had their fair share of sorrow and pain and deep despair, knowing that we are targeted more than any other people on the face of the earth because we are the children of God, and Lucifer hates us with a passion, because we were sent on earth to be the light bearer. Yes! To be the keeper of the flames of righteousness, being the little candle in the dark that keeps ablaze with love and mercy. Only to understand that keeping this eternal flame lit is no easy task. Still we were chosen to set the world on fire with the love of our Father at the helm. Did the Jews ever try to evangelize the rest of the world as John the Baptist did as a Jew? Was it given to us to sit on and keep for ourselves? These are very, very important question each one must ask them-selves, as there will be no starless crown in heaven. What Ishmael (the father of Islam) knows how to do best, is to evangelize, whether or not they get it wrong or right. Today it's not about religion but the intent of our hearts that will go on trial in front of The Ancient of Days, who is Righteous in All His Ways, being God and God Alone. Now that it's almost over what are we going to do with the little time that is allotted to us? Run and hide to preserves our lives or stand up and fight the good fight of faith.

At the beginning of Autumn, the Fall of 2016, I had a vision in which I saw a huge church, its interior painted in black as I was taken in the spirit to see this sad and grave revelation that is on our doorsteps. I was looking down from the ceiling, seemingly suspended in midair, so I was able to see the entire interior of the church. Everything in the church was painted black, from the altar to the pews and even the floors, yet I could see everything very distinctly. As I was there looking and wondering why the Lord would have taken me here in this empty dark and lonely church/place, like somewhere that needs a revival, plus a cleansing grace or a spiritual turn over, when Suddenly, out of nowhere a great gush of pure crystal clear water forcefully rushed from behind the pulpit, through the church and out the front door, like a mighty river. (I saw this twice in one night, waking up after the first time, then going back to sleep and having the exact same dream recur.) It was clear to me that The Lord is getting ready to cleanse the church of its hypocrisy, sexual immorality, with homosexuality and adultery at its peak. In a time when racism and prosperity religion, are pulling the church of God deeper into the murky waters of the earth. The bench warmers are getting ready to be spewed out of the mouth of God, for been lukewarm the worst place to be spiritually. It is now more than ever we must make our calling sure and start cleaning up our house and get it in order, which must start in us as individuals before we can lead our families and others to the foot of the cross, because judgment starts in the house of The Lord.

I understand this revelation to mean that there will be a great revival in the Middle East and around the world of men and women of Islamic and Jewish faith will come to know the essential truth that has been twisted by every religion on the face of the earth to fit their money chamber. But it is the promise that was given to our fathers starting in Abraham and passed on to, Isaac, and Jacob, and to Ishmael, the firstborn of our father who is also entitled to the very same love of The Most High.(you'll be surprise what was shown to me in a vision of "The Dark Cave "of which you will be the judge) We will come together and forgive one another before the great tribulation reaches its peak and ends in bloodshed and sorrow. Sadly, our eternal souls will be lost forever if we don't repent. I am not a scholar of biblical prophecy or religion. I'm just here to tell you what was shown to me before the disaster comes eastward.

The Truth of the matter is that we will not be saved without God on our side to deliver us from the claws of the adversary. Being a person of color and one of the children of Abraham is looked upon by some as a curse, but it is one of the greatest blessings in disguise. What most fail to realize is that God's children will always be oppressed by the enemy of God, Lucifer himself, camouflaged in the anger of men he uses against men. The ones with money are the ones who make the rules, while the ones with the knowledge make the laws, and they both join together to implement their rules and laws and suppress God's children. Without that kind of power on earth you can never win, no matter how physically strong you may be. Only the spiritual man can break out of such Luciferian bondage.

It is a known fact that money is power, and absolute power corrupts, with bloodshed always as its final goal and evil ambition. Look around you and you'll see who is behind it. This is the greatest tool they will use against the children of God. How many of us are willing to walk away from this money trail that will only lead us straight to the gates of hell? Many of you will find yourself at the place of no return in this time, waving the banner of "Making America Great Again". I pray that you will wake up and look up for once in your life and ask God the Most High to make your heart and spirit great again so that His will can be done in you, because we are going to need Him more than ever. It's going to be dreader than dread. Power and greed leads to, nowhere but to the gates of hell. Who is behind the power of corruption, hate and greed that always end in more bloodshed? Again it's Lucifer himself. The secret behind the secret is that this earthly secret is guarded with much secrecy (the accumulation of wealth) just as how they have guarded a nuclear arsenal so that it doesn't get into the wrong hands; it's the very same way wealth is guarded so that it doesn't get into the hands of the world's minorities. Another secret behind the secret which is a known fact is that all effort is made to keep wealth and knowledge out of our hands, and the few that are able to accumulate such wealth, are watched vigorously with every passing moment to find a way or loophole in the laws of the land to get it out of their hands. They have to be brainwashed and tested over and over again to make sure that they are not on the Lord's side. Do you think that it's a coincidence that people of color, the minorities of the world, will always be held on the edges of society? The ones who have made it to the top of the economic ladder are the ones that could not be stopped. The Jews are hated for their ability to accumulate wealth, and it's by Divine design that, though few in number, they control up to a third of the wealth of the entire world! For reasons known only to Him, I was privileged to learn from my Father Himself, The Lord God of The Most High, that I am of the tribe of Levi, and this is the greatest blessing and revelation ever given to me as mortal man. This was told to me almost 30 years ago not understanding how significant this was meant to be. It's only now I understood that it was to prepare me for these last days and what I must do to help you as my brothers and sisters connected directly to Abraham seed. I was sent to the house of the minority (of which I will show you in the vision when I was taken to heaven, and was also shown a glimpse of hell so that I could come and tell you of what they are both like). A true Levite life is not about earthly wealth, but as Moses and his brother Aaron walk for forty years through the wilderness, taking care of the spiritual aspect of the flock given to him to take care of by The Lord God of The Most High Himself, when He spoke to him on Mount Horeb. I must warn you that this is the last exodus (the spiritual movement of God's people) God hasn't forgotten us and this is the reason He sent a poor boy like me from humble beginning who have no ego in political or religious affairs (preachers and politicians, having the biggest ego) or want no position in this world but only to do the will of my Father. He didn't send someone of Jewish kin, He sent me someone who have been lost in the rubbles of Jamaica searching to know who I am and why I'm here on earth. For many, many years these are the thoughts that torment my soul. All I know was that I'm here for a specific reason, but I couldn't tell what it was. I thought at one time it was going to be music the passion of my life, but every-time I think of touring the Sabbath comes into being and I couldn't go against God's way in my heart though I'm perfectly flawed, but making up my mind to sin against The Lord God deliberately was not in my heart even though I have fallen a thousand times. it's the same way I feel about our soul's salvation. The accumulation of souls belongs to the Holy Spirit of who only can convict the hearts of man. I was sent as a reminder and one of the restorer of the breach. When my brothers and sisters speak of God's love and His everlasting mercy, this is what gives me the most joy. I want to be rich in love and mercy; it's the only thing I'm going to leave this world with plus my character. Everything else is vexation of the spirit. No one will be pulling a U-hall of trinkets behind them into heaven or hell, if you find yourself lucky and favored to be among the elect of God. If you find yourself among the downtrodden and the oppressed, count it as a blessing. Not everyone will come to know the essential truth, thinking themselves too significant to tell others about The Most

High, the same reason they deny Christ The Messiah because He came from humble beginnings.

"If Prince Williams Was Given Such Premonition…"

If Prince William of England were to announce that he has been given prophetic revelations from The Lord God of heaven and earth, how many of you in the hundreds of thousands each day would go out and try to get close to hear him speak of such revelation? The truth of the matter is that millions would flock to Buckingham Palace to hear him speak what was given to him to tell the world. But the all wise God will always be the mystery within the mystery, as He uses the foolish to condemn the wise. As in Corinthians 1:27 "But God used the foolish things of the world to shame the wise, and He uses the weak things of the world to shame the strong." The Essential truth was given to me as a reminder to the children of God what He spoke of when He said in John 10:16, "And other sheep I have, which are not of this fold: them also I must bring and they shall hear my voice; and there shall be one flock and one Shepard."

"A Leopard Never Change Its Spots"

Don't you realize that we have been scattered all over the world for over three thousand years? Long before Christ came on earth, the temple mount remained desolate and abandoned after the first destruction of the temple, so why the urgency to claim it now? Why is the Vatican so interested in it now? Consider what happened as events have unfolded along the natural path to the unknown, to the end of time. Though many romanticize the past that has led to the dictatorial power of the Vatican, let us not forget the Augustus Caesar of 63 BCE, who was depicted in Daniel's prophecies as having legs of iron and clay, signifying both strength and weakness. It was Augustus Caesar's rise to power that marked the beginning of the Fourth Kingdom, which has not faded into history but has lain dormant for centuries with the intent of regaining power, using Christianity as the catalyst. Make no mistake, the office of the pope of Rome is just another name for Caesar. Christianity is simply the façade and is being used in much the same way that Constantine used it to solidify his power as emperor of Rome once he realized Christianity was here to stay. It was the new pop culture, providing entertainment for the masses who thrilled at the gory demise of Christians in the arenas of Rome. Don't be fooled. The Vatican's intention is to reestablish the roman emperor. The difference this time is that it's not a European but the South American pope Francis from Peru, the first Jesuit priest to ever hold the office, who will usher in the end of time, starting with the great tribulation that is nearly upon us in 2017. But a leopard never changes its spots, and it's all about putting the antichrist, Lucifer himself, on the throne of David, right there on the temple mount in Israel, the very spot where the ark of the covenant once lay, in the most holy place. It is this pope that will take the Vatican to the brink of no return as it was prophesy as it will be done. I will show you in detail in "The Decoding of The Beast". The visions and dreams that the Lord God of The Most High has privy me to will paint a total different picture of which it will be totally up to you to decide. It is **freedom of choice** that is the handy work of God and what separate Him from all other gods.

Chapter 28

The President - Will Be Torn Between The Sabbath & The Sunday Law

I'll Leave You with One Parable to figure out

The Sabbath is going to play a major role in all of this that is to come, and the president is going to be torn between two forces. It's going to be between his son in law, (the man that his beloved daughter Ivanka Trump married to), Jared Kushner who is Jewish and one who keeps the sabbath (with their three beautiful children to the marriage) versus the vice president Mike Pence. There will be a roadblock for a moment, as one of the vision that was shown to me (when I was shown a prophetic vision a humongous star depicting Christ, just before His return. It was in 4 different colors, of which one was in blood. I was given the interpretation of a time period in amber color that must not be taken for granted or lightly, "whether or not I live to see it". There is a very important period on Gods prophetic time-clock before it turns to red which will be dreader than dread. It is here in this period in the great falling away many will be deceived, as well as many will turn to the essential truth and many more to eternal doom. I am not sure about a lot of things, but I will speak as the Spirit of The Most High leads me into all that I need to know, so that you in return can be aware. Ivanka who is now a Modern Orthodox – converted to Judaism, and loved been Jewish of all the beauty that the Sabbath brings. The great sense of peace and tranquility that comes with it is simple amazing like no other. It's only through experiencing it, you'll understand this in its entirety. The quality of time she gets to spend with family and friends on the Sabbath is quite beautiful and rejuvenating. People who have no clue of the Holy Sabbath and the joy it brings would be amazed at what they are missing. It's the day to be at peace with God and man, and there is a great blessing that comes with it, a sense of purpose. Still The Lord would never force anyman to keep it holy, even though it is holy. The Lord God of The Most High has put it aside as a very special day, where He is honored love and exalted in songs of praise to a Righteous and Holy God. It's no coincident that she has ended up in the white House with her father president Donald Trump as one of her father's advisor (assistant to the president) As her husband Kushner ended up as one of his key advisor (Senior Advisor to the president of the United States is his title) a very key position to be in serving the president of the most powerful country in the world. At the moment Kushner got the president ears, reason is he trusts him being the husband of his beloved daughter Ivanka, but it won't be for long. Peer -pressure will take him off his white horse that he so gracefully ride now, as Isreal get complacent, in this time having Kushner as a Jew in ever roundtable talk where Israel is concerned. I don't know if taking up the phone tomorrow and trying to get an interpreter to tell the president of Israel what was shown to me in vision will change anything. The first thing they are going to say is "who is this man?, never heard of him and what business he has in Jewish affairs," but here it is for you to see at least I warn you in "Writings on the Walls of Heaven". The deadly sting that has stung many great men before, mixed in a venomous potion will be given to the president, and he will drink from this cup, where absolute power is the objective. This will surly creep within the walls of the White House, which will have more secrecy, than Buckingham palace with its almost 300 years of secrets combined with the Kremlin of Russia put together. It's within these walls within the moment of the moment vice president Mike Pence will embrace a different agenda, bigger than life, that will make president Trump's ideas look like a country club in comparison to the throne of the most powerful villain on earth, waiting for this specific moment in time. Trump will resist for the love of his daughter, but without avail, as the hands of power will change, before the darkest hour of time creeps up on us. To change one's mind will be too late. President Trump who adores his grandchildren, will be put in the position of choosing a side, backed by popular demands, when the National Sunday –Law which is already on the books from 1610, before the first black man ever put foot in America as a slave. After the dust is settled with president Trumps connection to Russia, and the revelation of his tax return, just like the birther story with president Obama played out on the national stage a bit longer than he would like it to, but to no avail until he delivers or it buries him from what is within. Understanding that the law of nature is ruthlessly and relentlessly honest "whatsoever seed a man sowed, so shall he reap". The law of nature that governs the world is put in place by the hand of the Almighty God, long before the world was created. We serve a God who does not change; He is the same God of yesterday today and tomorrow. Whatever He says He will do, just as how He has sent me to come to you in this very important moment in time, of which the rest will be up to you. The question is, will president Trump denounce the religion of his daughter? Her new found Jewish faith in Judaism, adopted through her husband will be in question, versus the resurrection of the National Sunday Law which will be the relevant solution for a stable society that is hemorrhaging morally in every aspect of the American ideals. The question is will it stand the test of time and delay the fulfillment of Revelation 13, America giving the power to the Beast, who is cloaked in the robe of Catholicism under the banner of the Vatican of Rome? It is absolute power that corrupts.

Who will it be in the end to take hold of such coveted crown? Will it be China, or Russia who now shares the power struggle with America and whose ultimate ambition is to stand alone on the world stage of the world? But isn't there another power much darker and sinister, who is supposed to be larger than life, who has a different weapon of mass destruction, having another nuclear-code like nothing we've ever seen before? Without Christ intervening and shortening the time of earth's history, even the very elect of God would be lost. The things that I was shown in visions and dream, when The Lord God has opened my eyes to such mystery, will make your heart tremble. There will be a breakaway like a mystery movie playing out in the white house sooner than you think. Ivanka's heart will sink in agony, when she realizes that she will be the ace in the deck of cards, playing out in front of the American public and the world when she will have to choose. It's going to be, between her dearly beloved father versus her husband and kids that she adores. The dagger to her heart will only put the wolf that is carefully draped in sheep clothing one step closer to the throne. Will the world believe what they are witnessing when it starts playing out right in front of our very eyes? As the vice president will have the president ears as well as his son-in- law Kushner with his daughter in the middle. Ben Carson another Sabbath keeper in the white house with Pence with a total different agenda from the president. "To make America Great again" is the president most ferocious/aggressive agenda and if anyone gets in his way for such to come to fruition will become his number one enemy. For the vice president, its more rooted in subtle secrecy, with the intention of a total different agenda, which is the new world order, much bigger than life, which will be handed to him by the law and order president? Or will he have to fight building a darker path hoping Donald Trump will stumble in the dark? How it will be done is like nothing you've seen before.

Will it be by force, will Mike Pence secretly execute a plan for his own secret ambition making an enemy out of Trump as public enemy number one or by Divine design it will fall in place smoothly or will there be a blood bath to reach such ambitious endeavor ? (To be continued in – "We All Have Been Deceived") Vol. 2

Chapter 29

And What Will Become of The Sunday Law?

I'll Leave You with One Parable to figure out

"Did The Lord Say If You FEAR Me ....Keep My Commandment?"

The parable of the day is: Was it by Divine design that the 44th President; Barrack Obama was put on the hot seat, about the land of his birth? It was this topic that became the issue of the day in the consciousness of the American fabric for a moment and a day. Now the question is will the sheep dog eat the sheep or get stampeded by the sheep? The hand that feeds the hungry dog, often get bitten by the very same dog, how many bones will it take to fill its stomach, this time before it turns and eats him like a wolf? The real question is, have you ever seen a hungry wolf eaten by a dog? or is it the hungry dog that will eat the wolf this time?. The chaos in the white house will become the soap-opera of the century as the world will not be able to get enough of it .The secret behind the secret is that this very limelight will usher in a much darker and sinister reality that will catch us all off guard if you're not aware of what is to come. Was the Sabbath made for man, or man for the Sabbath? All of the above will come down to this very insignificant day as we make it out to be, but we will all see Something must give, who will it be?

The Sunday law: is already on the books as one of the religious enchantment, section 3, passed in Virginia in the year 1610. which read: "Every man and woman should repair (go habitually)in the morning to the divine service and sermons preached upon the Sabbath day (which they changed to Sunday – calling Sunday the Sabbath) and in the afternoon to divine, teaching the principles of Christian dogma and ethics, upon pain for the first fault, to lose their provision. Following; for the second and to lose their entire allowance for the whole week and also be whipt; and for the third (3rd) to suffer death. If they were killing people to keep the Sabbath day holy (which is the 4th commandment), like how they have killed millions in the past to keep Sunday sacred, I wouldn't be a part of it because it would tell me that The God that I come to know as my Father and friend would not be A God of his words, who gave man freedom of choice to choose. So right there and then it would not have matched up with the bible, and this I would have a problem with. It's not about what man tells me, it's always about what is there written in the bible, as to "Study to show thyself approve a work-man should never feel ashamed rightly dividing the word of truth" 2nd Timothy 2:15. The very same words that Yashuah The Christ used to conquer Satan the Devil when He said to this culprit they call Lucifer when tempted by him. The Lord God of The Most High turn to him and said "It is written!!" Even before He said man shall not live by bread alone, but by every word proceeded out of the mouth of God" Christ means every word and not the ones that are twisted and change to fits one secret agenda.

Look at all the apostles who have paid dearly with their lives, of which none of us is exempt, Just like the reformers of the 'Dark Ages' and millions who followed The Lord and the holy scripture, instead of the pope of Rome, they were burn to the stakes. Their charges were going against the Catholic Church, using their conscience and the word of God from the Holy Scriptures as their guide and badge of honor. How easy we forget the harrows of yesterday. Millions putting their trust in Jesus Christ until the very moment when they strike the match to start the bon-fire that would take them into eternity knows that what they have done only The Spirit of God could help them through it. It will happened again and this time it will be the very last time just before the return of "Yashua" Jesus Christ The Messiah, who I called affectionately **"The Lord God of The Most High"** The Only Begotten of The Father ….The Ancient of Days…… What were they guilty of? They were guilty of trusting God and God Alone, and not putting their trust in fallible, sinful man including the pope and the preachers and teachers, that are driven by power and ego and greed; yes!! men of ego who wants to be worshipped. Fallible, unrighteous humans as we all are want to take the place of God as their father the devil craved worship. Put your trust in no man on earth who are only human, as we all are, but learn to trust God and God Alone. It is now time to search our hearts for the truth, because the children of God know the truth, because His sheep knows His voice. As David had said to the Lord, when he was going through rough times in the valley of the shadow of death, of which he feared no evil, because he knew that God was with him. Still he would say these most profound words to his Father The Most High "Rewrite your laws on the fleshy tablets of my heart that I will not sin against Thee" It is time for the children of God to come back to the essential truth ……… **The Great Falling away must come first which is here before our probation closes.**

All that is to come will come, make no mistake. You and I will not be able to stop the sea of events that will knock on our doors, all you must do is to get ready for it. 1st Timothy 4 - "Now the Spirit speaketh expressly, that in the latter times, some shall depart from the faith, giving heed to seducing spirits and doctrine of devils;

Speaking lies in hypocrisy; having their conscience snared with a hot iron. If this was not inevitable that we would stray away from the truth, the disciples of Jesus who have walked with him and hear Him speak to the hearts of men and teach them(as His disciples) many things. Timothy a disciple of Christ went on to say "I charge thee therefore before God, and The Lord Jesus Christ, who shall judge the quick and the dead at His appearing and His kingdom; preach the word; be instant in season, out of season rebuke, exhort with all long suffering and doctrine. For the time will come when they will not endure sound doctrine; but after their own lust shall they heap to themselves teachers having itching ears; And they shall turn away their ears from the truth, and shall be turned into fables. But watch thou in all things, endure afflictions, do the work of an evangelist, make full proof of thy ministry. 2nd Timothy 1-5 The things that the Lord God reveals to me sometimes only make me smile in awe of such wonderful love He has for me to even allow to hear things that is only spoken of in the Holy Bible of the men and women He chooses to reveal himself to of whom some He have called His friends, some His messenger and some His prophets. I considered myself to be a humble servant of His who is also my only friend. Strange as it may sound, it's true ,because I put my trust in no man on earth. Once I did and have been let down so many times, until I learned to trust God and God Alone. The day He called me by my name, out of the heavens of heavens was the day that changed my life forever. I was called many names as a boy growing up in the hills of Glendevon ,but The Lord called me Mutti, (a name given to me by my dad)

Thirty seven and going on to almost forty years ago God called me by this very name, there must be a reason why He called me by this name, there must be a reason why this strange name was given to me, a very rare one indeed. Only two more people in my life time I ever heard with this name, Mutti Perkings. Just as how He had sent his holy angel to come down to earth and sing for me, a very familiar song written by man that I never knew angels could sing. Who are we as fallible men to decide the things of the infallible ONE?

Again did The Lord say if you Fear Me Keep My commandment? Or did he say "If you Love Me Keep My Commandment?"

Chapter 30

The Vision- I Heard an Angel Sing.......

Who would believe that angels would sing the songs of sinful mortal men? It was this moment as graphic and real as in real-time it seemed ,when I experienced one of the most breath-taking and mystical moment of a lifetime. It was here I understood the handy work of our Creator. It was also in this vision, I understood that everything that happened had to do with the spiritual aspect of our lives a little better . I came to the understanding without a doubt, that the word of The Most High God are given to men and women He chooses to reveal Himself to in inspirational words of wisdom , the hymns of praise written in songs of inspiration over the years has made foot-prints on many of our hearts and most powerful of them all the book of all books the Holy Bible that I over-heard so many so-called scholars, calling and treating the Holy- Bible arbitrarily, as if it's just a bunch of illogical stories, more symbolical than being pragmatic. Most of those I overheard does it to show off to their friends and colleagues how learned or smart they are because men love the glory and approval of men rather than the approval of God ....knowing that the Spirit of God gave us His word for our benefit. As if they have the power to debunk spiritual things just because we have freedom of choice, and we can do it if we choose to knowing quite well that most of the time it's just to prove a point, forgetting that everything that has a beginning also has an ending. We can always continue to play with words all who claim to be atheist, agnostic and all the others.

There will always be consequences for our actions; whether good or bad. It's quite amazing how men often think that they can score a point against our Creator for shunning the words of the bible, calling it a little story book. When the bible is more practical, rather than theoretical considerations. I often listen to the silly –wise men, trying to impress upon their peers how learned they are, not knowing that the things of God given to sinful fallible men to give to His children, little do some of us know that it is a privilege to be able to hear God words that He has spoken thousands of years ago to His patriarch and prophets also His messengers and to our minds and hearts read Gods words for ourselves way beyond our comprehension as fallible men always think that they understand the mystery of God when He only reveal himself to those He loves. Do we think that we can buy Gods love with our money?

Do we really think that we can have conversations with The Most High without Him inviting us to come? It is our hearts that decide who gets the invitation and who do not, because" blessed are the pure in heart for they shall see God". Those He chooses to talk to in dreams and visions is because their hearts are pure, thou they might be perfectly flawed. It is He who have to choose us we cannot buy our way into His presence, like these clergy men and women selling feel good religion would want you to believe . Just like the catholic priest and popes of yesteryears who called themselves the vicar of God selling indulgencies to the highest bidders.

The true word of God are really written by inspired men and women of His. Those who try to take His word lightly will regret every moment of such mockery on the most powerful pieces of literature ever written on the face of the earth given to man.

Moses was the first chosen one of God to whom such history

wrapped in mystery of the world was revealed.

The Lord God would speak into his mind and spirit the very words that he has written in the Torah known as the books of Geneses, Exodus Leviticus, Numbers just to name a few as others would follow . It was David (Gods beloved) who wrote the psalms which mostly are songs of praises to his Heavenly Father and King who he addressed as The Most High God and often called Him JAH.........

In the highest adoration he gave praises to The Creator of the universe like none other before him. This vision will tell its own story ......

As I retire to bed fell asleep in the middle of the night this is what I saw..........un-deserving though I be.

The Vision

And I found myself at my home, where I grew up in Glen-Devon, and I was having a conversation with my mother. We were talking standing at the back door of the room I used to share with my brothers as a kid. From there you could see the beautiful mountain slopes. They are not high, but the contours of the hills and the valley make the landscape so much more interesting. I miss it and yearn to go back every chance I get. Despite the den of thugs it has become, but as always there's nothing like home. Our house was on a hill, just a stone's throw away from Blood Lane down below, a place that got its name from the volatility of the people. Though you can still find beautiful people living there, they are few and far between. I stood there as an adult watching the rooster in our yard chasing all the hens and rivals who one day would come up against him (if he doesn't get cooked for a Sunday dinner). The little chicks ran behind the mother hen as she scratched here and there between the rocks to find little bugs or worms to feed them. As I was observing the surroundings that I love and had missed so much, suddenly I heard coming from over the mountain slope the most beautiful voice that made shivers run up my spine.

I turned and looked up to the hills where the voice was coming from in jaw-dropping amazement of what I was hearing. Sitting a distance across the hill is a huge white reservoir on top of the mountain, where we fetched water as kids when we were experiencing summer droughts. When I was a little boy, we would all go up with our pots and pans and buckets, and it would be one of our greatest joys to bathe in the cool rushing water as it gushed out, by hundreds of gallons at a time, and we were happy as a lark. Sometimes months passed with no water coming up to our mountain. Reason is the pipes are usually dry in the summer times, and we'd have to wait for the rain to fall, and live without water when it didn't, we would have to wait sometimes for weeks for the government to send trucks carting water to help us out. So when the reservoir was full, we were always grateful and would haul home enough to serve us as long as possible, not knowing when we would have water again if the rain didn't fall.

There is a little church painted in white sitting on top of Reservoir Hill, and you can see it from miles away. When I heard the voice coming from the top of the mountain, it echoed across Glen Devon, and everything that had breath stood still. The rooster stopped running after the hens, and the mother hen and its little chicks all stopped at the same time and looked up like nothing they've heard before . The barking dog fell silent and turned its head towards the mountain as the most beautiful voice I have ever heard or ever been heard on the face of the earth sang in the most melodic, high-pitched tones. It was pure and had a holy resonance to it, calm and smooth, in total jaw dropping amazement; and as I looked to see where it was coming from, gazing in astonishment and great curiosity, everything came to a perfect standstill. Suddenly, I was carried away in the Spirit, and was taken to the top of the hill from which this mysteriously beautiful and melodic voice echoed over the mountain slopes. And what I saw literally blew my mind. As I stood there in awe, looking upon this graceful, beautiful, mysterious being, I realized that I was in the presence of one of my Father's holy angels. Seraphim, I thought was the right word. This glorious being was singing a very familiar song, one that my mother often sings on Friday evenings, after the sun has set to usher in the holy Sabbath when the children of The Lord God of The Most High around the world sing praise and glory in worship to His righteous and Holy Name.

What I saw was more than my tongue can explain and a beautiful sight indeed to behold—a white horse, standing gracefully on the hilltop by the little church, on four strongly muscled legs, like a white stallion from the land of the Eternal One. From its neck down to its tail was simple perfection, the simplest of beauty human eyes can ever behold. Its beautiful poise said that it had sung many songs of praise before its Maker and King. As I stood there and gazed at its beauty in amazement, I realized that from its neck upward it was like a man, strong and handsomely built, yet more than man, with beautifully toned muscles from his waist upward ... handsome and with one of the greatest voices imaginable.

This beautiful angelic being was standing in the church yard singing: "O day of rest and gladness ... Oh day of joy and light ... Oh balm of care and sadness ... most beautiful, most bright ... On Thee the high and lowly, who bend before THY throne ... sing Holy, Holy, Holy, to The Eternal ONE." Half horse, half man ... Thou Art a Port protected from storms around us rise ... a garden intersected with streams of paradise ... Thou Art a Cooling Fountain in life's dry dreary sand … from Thee like Pisgah's mountain, We view our promised land. "I had only ever heard of such beings in mythology and stories that supposedly have no merit, and here My Heavenly Father made me privy to another phenomenon, one that I am not even worthy to behold, and still He showed me all these things. I asked myself once again "what have I done to deserve this?" the answer I guess will only come if I am faithful unto the end. meaning of what I was seeing as I gazed upon this being's beauty in amazement.

As he sang and I looked on this great wonder of God's creation, I couldn't help but bow my heart in Godly fear and adoration to my Father The King of Kings and Lord of Lords, knowing that I am one of His own, just because of the little things that He has done for me, or allowed me to get glimpses of. Oh! What a Mighty God we serve. As I was there gazing on its beauty of perfection, and the greatest voice I have ever heard sing praises to The Most High, I was then carried away back in the Spirit, and I awoke from the vision. Everything was exactly as when I had left and every living creature had stopped what it was doing and stood still.

I was placed there right in the presence of this heavenly being, and what I heard and saw was simple and amazingly great to hear. The angel singing the song that mortal man wrote made me realize that some of His children, the ones He chooses to reveal himself to, are without a doubt writing under the inspiration of a Holy God, as the Holy Bible was written by inspired men and women of God. "Oh Day of Rest and Gladness" is one of my mother's favorite songs, one that she taught us to sing to usher in the Holy Sabbath day that men now on earth want to abolish and will be the turning point in the great tribulation. Don't take my word for it you will see it all played out in front of you.

Do you really think that my heavenly Father sent His angel to sing for just singing sake? Think again my friends . It was much , much bigger than that and much, much more significant than anything that I have ever been privy to since these dreams and visions began.

This was about the significant of the covenant He made between us as His children and people. The promise He had made to Abraham that he will be the father of many nation and his seed will be like the sand of the sea here is the one significant proof for their distinction among men here on earth. It was never about circumcision even though that was important ,but the keeping of the holy Sabbath is without a doubt the circumcision of the heart.

This is the reason why He said "REMEMBER THE SABBATH DAY TO KEEP IT HOLY" it is so significant my dear friends let no man fool you.

By the TIME you realize that the New World order is here, you will realize that it will be based on this very commandment, the 4th commandment, but by then it might be eternally too late.

If the new world order is not based on the national Sunday law which will call for the abolishing of the 4th commandment then look for all these books and burn them and block my name out of your memory like I've never existed and was the one given this assignment to write "The Black Books of Moses ....with The Rise of The Tribulation President the first volume.

If the pope of Rome will not ask for the abolishment of the 4th commandment giving credence to the national Sunday law, then I have been leaning on my own understanding and was not writing under Divine guidance.

All of Gods messengers prophets and patriarchs have spoken

about this. It's nothing new. All that The Lord God of The Most High did was to send me another confirmation just like when Moses saw Him write it with His very fingers.

He now sent one of His holy angels to give me the last and final analogy of its importance as it will without a doubt separate the sheep from the goats.

Truth of the matter is that I'm only doing what I was sent to do. I really don't know how it will play out The spirit of The Lord is here telling me as I write this final part of the Rise of The tribulation President "that it will be much too late by the time they realize if you don't take heed now while there is still time."

For an heavenly being to come and sing this holy and righteous song inspired by God Himself both melody and lyrics; can't you tell that something is very, very significant about this? Can't you tell that man will be judged by this very dogma, this set of principle laid down by God Himself.

Why would this 4th commandment be the only law out of the ten that man want to abolish so bad if it was not significant. This one commandment is incontrovertibly true and will be the deciding factor at the end of the world as we know it. Hearing it in vision, telling me that there is a covenant between God and man, and this is the reason why He said, "REMEMBER THE SABBATH DAY TO KEEP IT HOLY." It was never enforced by anything other than pure love. He said "If you love me keep my commandment". Don't be deceived by these devils that tell you the Sabbath is abolished, for they are working under the influence and darkness of their father, the devil.

To hear an angel sing one of mortal men melody of praise to The Most High is one of the greatest experiences ever given to sinful man. Unworthy though I am, The Lord sent His angel to sing a song of praise so I could hear the beauty of His eternal grace and love. It was not far from where I used to write my little songs of praise to the Lord when I first learned how to compose. I was only 10 years old when I wrote my first song, and by the time I was 12 or 13 years old, mother always had to call me in the morning to come and have something to eat, before I got an upset stomach from not having something warm in it. I would sit right under this huge birch- wood tree in our backyard, right in front of our outdoor toilet, and I would write my songs of inspiration for hours as the Holy Spirit would come and visit. It is really an honor to have heard God's angel sing, a privilege accorded to few men on earth. At the end of the day remember that it was much, much more significant than the most beautiful voice ever heard, the secret behind the secret is that everything that had life that I could see in front of me acknowledge what they heard. I pray that you will do the same. This is not about force, but only out of love can we please The Most High God. If you're wise you will take heed .Remember we cannot serve God The Most High out of fear but out of love only. Again The Lord said "If you love me ….Keep my commandment".

Chapter 31

The Beginning of Sorrow Is Upon Us and the Media Will Help to Decide It

President Trump is still a Democrat at heart playing hardball to that the U.S. constitution will soon be a thing of the past. The media put him on top of the political arena but he will silence it through creeping compromise backed by the demands of his base that will not see anything he does as being wrong. The truth of the matter is that what is about to take place on earth is not an illusion. Don't forget what he has promised to the people that elected him to the presidency. And who can blame them for being swayed, when the moral code of America was on its very death bed as gay marriage became law in this country that was built upon Christian principles, this country that could have chosen rule by an autocrat or king when George Washington was elected in 1789. We are seeing and will continue to see marches and demonstrations in the streets of America and around the world, but the secret behind the secret is that there has to be great unrest in order to justify the laws that will be enacted to secure the new world order, including the Sunday law. Our safety will be used as the platform by design that will help to implement laws passed under Barrack Obama as the 44th president that set the stage for everything that is to come. The secret behind the secret is that all of this is much bigger that politics—much, much bigger than the GOP and the Democrats all put together. What you and I fail to understand is that this is God's time, even though every person will still have the freedom of choice to do whatever he or she wants to do. The sad thing is that the fate of so many has already been sealed. The year of jubilee will be over by the end of 2017, and the spring of 2018 will be a new beginning as you'll see the true path to the end of the world as we know it. It's going to be sad for many, but some of us still stand a chance because God's love is still more powerful than His wrath. Yes! His love is much more powerful than His anger, and it's up to you and me to take advantage of these final moments in time as the last animals are about to enter the ark. Once that door is closed, and sealed by unseen hands, those outside will be left to stand and stare.

We have reached this pivotal moment in time and though we will not understand it all, we must listen to reason and make up our minds before it's eternally too late. It will soon be almost impossible to come and go without a conscious checkpoint, though at first it won't be physical. But I assure you that what the Lord God has shown me in vision will come to pass. It was in a prophetic dream given to me in the summer of 2016 that I saw people of all races and ethnicities marching through rioting crowds in the streets of America. What was surprising to be about this prophetic dream is that what happened next was unbelievably swift and direct. Please don't take these things that I'm saying to you lightly. The fact is that most people are living in an illusion and do not hear what they're supposed to hear but rather what they want to hear and see what they want to see, not what they're supposed to see. That is how this presidency will take them all by storm. It is through this presidency that the NRA will become a thing of the past, and Trump himself does not even know that he is simply fulfilling a role that has to be fulfilled by being his own self. He's no more than an actor who has no control over the script. He will stay in character right up to the point that he hands the lead role to his co-star, Mike

Pence, who is going to hit the ball out of the playfield, and nothing and no one will be able to stop what will happen, though many will try without avail. Lucifer's greatest deception is confusion. Once he can create that kind of atmosphere and you and I buy into it, he wins. Just like so many different ideas of who God is and what His real name is that people will argue about it for hours upon hours and days upon days that turn into unfulfilled years, not understanding that it's the intent of our hearts that God looks at. He knows each and every one of us, and the truth of the matter is that most of the things we put great emphasis on will not matter in the end. What will matter is "If you love me keep my commandment." This is what is paramount, and for this The Lord God of the Most High would turn and say, "Blessed are the pure in heart for they shall see God."

The secret behind the secret is that the Antichrist craves worship and praise and glory, because he wants to be like the Most High. The ambition of the new world order is to rebuilt the temple of Jerusalem, where they can offer blood sacrifice again, but who will get the honor and glory in the new temple that they intend to build? No one but Lucifer, the great abomination against The Lord God of The Most High, defying the life and death of Jesus Christ, as if His blood is not sufficient for all. Again Remember, Lucifer cannot make this happen on his own. Human beings have to assist him in this ambitious undertaking, the darkest in earth's history. This is how you will understand how limited this being that is called Lucifer is. Without you giving him the power he is nothing. He had to work through man to accomplish his goals on earth. Humans give him power, just as the media and political pundits give power to the masses or take power from them. This makes it essential that they be very careful about where their loyalty lies, or where their conscience is. If their first concern is for ratings they are in the same boat as Rush Lambert and the other GOP loyalists who misconstrued a lot of the narratives from the Obama administration and created a Donald Trump. I was most impressed by Mike Barnicle's Daily Beast article of March 13, 2016, in which he speculated on what Bobby Kennedy would have said to Trump. "Trump's words do not inspire his crowds. They anger. He does not encourage. He aggravates. He does not appeal to our strength. He focuses on the weakest elements of human nature, envy, anxiety, and apprehension of what might happen to America without him at the helm.

He is not a bad man. He is just one more public man who thinks and believes that each image of himself in the mirror reflects an individual greatness no one else owns. This, of course, makes him not that much different from the many who have ever announced for the presidency." And it continues ... what is missing on the weekend of 3/13/16, Donald Trump was revving up his supporters, testing the waters to see their true loyalty towards him. Like any man with ambition to become an emperor, he had to first have the people on his side before going against the establishment—the GOP establishment in this case. He figured out how to ambush them, and they realized that they were vulnerable, and Trump, a shrewd businessman who has dealt with some of the most corrupt minds, was able to manipulate the entire process to his advantage. The GOP has been hijacked and is scrambling to figure out how to take back the plane and try to land it safely. But it's much too late. Trump is in the pilot seat now, with no experience as a pilot, but he knows how to put the plane on autopilot, fueled by his ego, which he has in abundance. This fulfills Rome's great desire to see the American political process held hostage putting their most coveted ambition within reach.

Once Donald Trump realized that he can get away with saying

anything and that everything he does is forgivable, many believed he would start speaking more rationally and become presidential. But he continues to display his true nature. As Maya Angelou said, "When a person tells you who they are you must believe them." Many Americans agree with Donald Trump deep within their hearts, though some are less enthusiastic about the idea of making America great again. (We've heard similar messages from the great dictators of Europe.) Millions of Americans went against their own conscience in voting for him, though they find him personally repugnant." When asked by his disciples, "What shall be the sign of thy coming, and of the end of the world?" Jesus offered these prophetic words: "Take heed that no man deceive you. For many shall come in my name, saying, I am Christ; and shall deceive many. And ye shall hear of wars and rumors of wars: see that ye be not troubled: for all these things must come to pass, but the end is not yet. For nation shall rise against nation, and kingdom against kingdom: and there shall be famines, and pestilences, and earthquakes, in divers places. All these are the beginning of sorrows" (Matthew 24:6-8).

.....The mystery of the secret behind this secret is that this part of the prophesy has already been fulfilled, beginning with the destruction of Jerusalem and the scattering of the ten lost tribes of Israel across the earth, and in the two World Wars and all of the conflicts since. The invention of nuclear weapons by the United States of America gave us the power to destroy the world. But it was God, knowing the power of men, that allowed us to create and wield such destructive weapons of mass destruction. And the prophecy will be fully realized as Rome regains its power, and the unrest in America under President Trump and around the world is a part of the plan of salvation that must be played out.

Chapter 32

The Great Mysterious Check-Mark of Doom - by the Unseen Hands of God

"Is this the Window of Probation Closes?"

In the middle of the night after a long day of writing, working on this urgent assignment given to me by the Lord God Himself, after I retired to bed, not long after I put my head on my pillow I fell into a deep sleep. As I sleep The Lord visited me and showed me things that is to come that sometimes makes my heart cringe. This particular night in the Autumn of 2016 was no different but was very different, in the sense of the premonition and the nature of such, knowing the importance of such revelation given to me at times or as often as He deems it fit, puts deeper in humility of heart to be a vessel of where he can come and abide, and speak to me in these last troublesome days on earth, that will only get worse by the seconds. Tonight was no different and all I can do as His humble servant is to write what I saw, so that I can give it back to you and let you decide. This is what I saw in the check-mark of doom. I found myself on this road walking swiftly out of a city I could see behind me. In front of us was a long road that goes up a hill as I could see its winding turns going West. We were walking and I was looking ahead, wondering where we were going with all these people (though it's a handful) still I don't know them. The only person I recognize in the little handful of people was a friend of mine who I called Charlie (one of my co-producer and engineer for a little recording studio I have) There was something strange about him walking in the kind of crowd I thought it was. Knowing how he thinks having much philosophical conversation over the years, and him having an agnostic view of God and religion would make me think twice (which is as agnostic believes – is the philosophical view that the existence of God or the Supernatural are unknown and unknowable).

He would be the last person I would ever expect to be among these people I happened to find myself among which is such a blessing, but it seems somehow our conversation over the years pays off (this little body of people are, the children of God who, were inspired to leave the city while there was still time). What was strange is that Charlie always carries his nap-sack with him wherever he is going, and for some strange reason this time his hands were empty as if we had left the city behind in a rush, trying to get out before the abomination of desolation began. Then suddenly the Spirit of The Most High beckons to me to look up! And I did look up in the sky, and what I saw was without a doubt one of the most graphic and revealing vision of the very end and final days on earth. As I was walking steering into the mysterious heavens, what I saw was nothing unusual as the sky was blue and the sun was shining, just like a regular day on earth, but somehow the fact that I was told to look I kept looking. I was able to look straight into the sun, which was strange as if The Lord God has turned down its brightness so I could see.

As I gazed into the sky what I saw next was indeed nothing I would expect, like nothing I have seen before. I saw something very mysterious happen to the sun; it was like a pale mist came over it which made it seem unusually somber.. Reason I was able to look upon it without been blinded by the light. As I was looking and walking at the same time (running from whatever we were moving away from, that seems like a sense of urgency) then out of nowhere came something like an unseen hand starting closing the curtains of heaven just like a window been draped, as if to pull the eternal curtains of heaven over the shining sun with both hands as if to say **"The Window of Probation"** has been closed. Is this what it really is? I really don't know if that's what it means, I can only write what The Spirit of the Lord God of heaven and earth has shown me, as I always try to write precisely as I saw it. What I know for sure is that something has come to an END………God help us!. I'm pondering to myself this is surreal "Did I just saw something like a mysterious unseen hand veiled the sun as two window curtain closing, meeting each other in the center with precision (as God is precise in everything He does) that covers across the sun and the sun is no more, did I just really saw this?" I asked myself. The very spot where the sun was, I saw the most amazing thing ever on the face of the earth happened in front of my very eyes.

I saw the unseen hand of God put the biggest Check –Mark right in the very spot of where the sun once was, just moments ago, as if to say **"It Is DONE or It Is OVER"**. As I stood there for a moment waiting to see what next, within the same moment, I saw something even more bold and peculiar and I must say strange and mysterious indeed, starts unfolding, as I watched in great amazement with Godly fear I realized something very peculiar as if the sun was not under the cloud but realized that the check mark by the hand of God replace the sun like a permanent seal, as if signaling an end to something very significant, like a mark made by a teacher ticking off answers on a final exam in the last class needed for graduation. I saw it as a tick of the celestial pen checking off God's chosen people, in the final sealing of the saints on earth. It seems to me The Lord God of The Most High is showing me glimpses of the final approval. That check mark also can signal God's confirmation that seals the fate of man like "It Is Done!".

Who would believe that I've been shown these things in a vision, which I thought was only for righteous men?

As I kept looking, out of nowhere comes the same unseen fingers and my jaw fell to the ground as I watched in great astonishment, and incredulity. I could only open my mouth in awe without a word. Speechless I must admit. I scratched my head saying to myself "I read about these things in the Holy Bible, and here I am after all these thousands of years The Lord God is now showing me these things? "To see the heaven comes alive in these visions is no joke and not for every eyes to see, all I could say is "Oh my God!" Stunningly as I gazed upon this mysterious event, I saw the imaginary finger of God once more (just like the fingers that wrote the ten commandments on the two tablets of stone, as Moses stood in front of The Lord God of The Most High and looked on in great amazement I suppose), just as how I now witness these writing on the walls of heaven. . The unseen finger of The Lord God started writing something on the right side of the humongous check-mark, and these are the very words that came from the finger of God "**THE MOMENT OF MY COMING IS HERE**" As I looked on with Godly fear, wondering what on God's earth am I witnessing, or what is The Lord showing me, it suddenly vanished out of the sky. As soon as that vanished, once again the mighty finger of God started writing again, this time underneath those very words came the writing on the face of heaven. Here I am in Godly fear asking myself, as the event unfolds and I don't know what to expect next, is anyone seeing what The Great and Mighty God is showing little unworthy me?, I just could not believe what I was seeing. What I saw next as my eyes were glued on this great revelation given to me and written by my Fathers own hand, I then saw written in white on the face of heaven **"The moment is Now!"**

This time just a bit faster, again I repeat as it is important that I say it twice, He wrote these very words "**THE MOMENT IS NOW**" Then as soon as it was written, the writing disappeared, as I was calling to Charlie (who was walking about five feet away from me) to look up in the sky to see if he could see what I was seeing, but he was focused on getting away from what we left behind, trying to focus on where we were going it seems, and didn't stop to look up not once. He simply kept walking, as if his mind was in a different place as we try to keep up, following the people that were in front of us—not a huge crowd, but only a handful of people on a road going from north to west. As Christ has said, "pray that our flight is not in the wintertime or on the Sabbath day" (Matthew 24:20). When I looked back into the heavens it was gone**; seems to be a onetime warning.** "Surely Yahuah The Lord God of The Most High will do nothing, but He revealeth His secrets unto His servants the prophets" Amos 3;7 I know it might sounded a bit raw and unfiltered but I must tell you what The Lord God of The Most High has shown to me………..The time is now my friends!! there is no more signs to look for if we keep on looking for signs we are going to be lost. It is in this very moment that we must get our house in order to meet The Lord God of The Most High on His great and mighty return.

Isn't it amazing that Jesus Christ, The Messiah and The only Begotten Son of The Most High, would speak of the importance of the Sabbath in the context of times of tribulation which He tell us would come at the end of time? It is very, very significant. The secret behind the secret of Paul's claim to the first day of the week is ludicrous. My question is, did Paul really write these things in the bible or is this one of the greatest deceptions of the Church of Rome—in tampering with the word of God? It is time we start searching the scripture diligently for ourselves, and stop listening to these fake preachers who have hidden agendas, which is to rejoin the Vatican of Rome, been promised more power I assume debunking the sacrifice of the great reformers. Just like it was in the beginning so shall it be in the end. Everything has a season and this moment in life is the end of the road. The truth of the matter is that it is over. The rise of the tribulation president is about to take this world in a tail spin, like nothing you've seen before. One of these mornings you're going to wake up and asked yourself "what happened to the great America, the land of the brave and the free?" It will no longer be here, as it used to be.

Every man will be subject to a different order, and will be moved around like cattle 'as the New World Order take president. It's coming folk's weather or not we like it, it's a must. The Lord God of The Most High has just shown me that it's over, and it's time we get our house in order before its eternally too late. The stage is already set for everything that is to come, come to fruition.

Chapter 33
What We Don't Understand

It's Time to Surrender to God Repent because the Kingdom of God Is Now!!

What we don't understand as sinful humans is that The Lord God of The Most High will not wait until we are ready, in our own time, to repent of our sins and come to Him. What we fail to realize as humans is that there is a cut off time for every person under the sun, and it's not us who decides when that time is, but God Himself. Again, it is the intent of our hearts that is most important to God, not the actuality. If it were the actuality, then it would be impossible for the great reformers of the world to be saved—men like Martin Luther and John Huss and John Calvin, to name a few. The fourth commandment was buried, abolished under Catholicism, and The Lord God of The Most High raised up these great reformers in a time when the pope of Rome was king on earth. To topple such an establishment would have taken more than courage; it required the hand of God. It is those who keep the commandments of God and the testimony of Jesus Christ who will inherit eternal life. It was with purity of heart that these men exposed the work of the devil hiding behind Christianity, cloaked in the deceptive banner of Catholicism governed by the Vatican. It is the covenant between God and man that those who do His work will be saved. The great reformers will be exempt because they were chosen to break the chain of the great deception. It was William Miller who was chosen in 1844 to shed light on the prophecy of Daniel 2 to bring about fulfillment one of the greatest biblical prophecies, which is Ezekiel 37. The cleansing of the

Sanctuary described in Daniel 2 had to happen before the children of Israel could return to the Promised Land as foretold in Ezekiel 37, and the children of Israel in the United States were enslaved until they were freed in 1861 by President Lincoln, selected by The Most High God to bring Ezekiel 37 to fruition. It is no coincidence that Lincoln's first name was Abraham. He was a prophetic president, as President Obama was and President Trump will be. Abraham Lincoln trusted God in one of the most devastating periods in the history of America, when blood ran like water, as it did to fulfill the liberation of Israelites held in bondage around the world.

The Lord guided President Lincoln with wisdom and understanding to steer the newest of world powers through the atrocities of the Civil War. Who would have ever believed that this young country would grow up to become the place of refuge and the beacon of hope for the world? And who would have believed that she would grow up to become the foremost power on earth, a power to be reckoned with? No one but The Most High could have orchestrated everything to put in place the pieces of the great mysterious puzzle for the final countdown of earth's history, starting with the great tribulation. America has now grown up, as the Lord has shown me the vision of how she will exercise her military might. The vision of the end of the world with nuclear missiles shooting out of the earth in rapid speed showed me great devastation taking place on American soil. The Lord God of The Most High appearing to me in the first vision also was here in America, representing the great power of this country.

The four different manifestations of this very vision often make me wonder if it they represent America in its four stages. And when The Lord God of The Most High said to me, "It is you," the truth of the matter is that this is not about me, but about this very last message that was given to me to deliver to all who will listen. It is America that will deal the final blow to civilization and end the world as we know it. She is the last great power on earth, and everything that The Lord has shown me in vision points to her as the one that will finish it all, though some Jewish scholars claim it's going to be in Israel. This might be true as far as the battle of Armageddon is concerned, but it will be America that will be the deciding factor that makes it happen. America has to let go the children of Israel who had been enslaved here for 400 years. All of God's children must be free to make their own decision before the end comes. Here we are as the children of Israel scattered all over the earth as a symbol of His truth and righteousness. The earth is getting ready for the day of jubilee, and after that—God help us.

It would have been a hundred years from the Great Disappointment of 1844 to 1944, when over 6 million European Jews had perished and over 60 million lives, a third of the world's population at the time, were lost, but still it was not Armageddon. It was totally impossible, for Jesus Christ to return in 1844 because with the children of Israel in turmoil and scattered all over the world, all of the prophecies that had to be fulfilled to bring Ezekiel 37 to fruition had not yet been realized. The Lord said heaven and earth shall pass, but not one word shall come back void. This simply means that everything He said would happen will happen exactly as He said. Some of the visions He has given to me are still a mystery to me, but my job is to deliver them, as all of the prophets and messengers of old did. It's not about me, but about Him who has sent me in this most crucial time in earth's history. Finding ourselves in a strange land, by the rivers of Babylon, where we sat down and wept when we remembered Zion, required from us a song. But how can we sing a redemption song in a strange land?

FOR THE ELECT SAKE.......

Chapter 34

For the Sake of the Elect and the Intent of the Heart

"Some Men Build Walls While Others Build Bridges"

If you take nothing else away from this book I want you to remember this little passage because it may change your life forever. Some may dismiss it, but you would understand if you were a seeker of the truth and had experienced what I experienced as a boy. Age has nothing to do with knowing the sacred truth if you are of being of Abraham's true bloodline and in relationship with Christ The Only Begotten Son of God, which is the only thing that is important now and will be important at the end of life's journey. Some men build walls to keep God's children out of His great plan for man's salvation, while other build bridges to help them to come over and find the truth. I'm one of those people sent to help tear down the walls of lies and deception, replacing them with bridges to the essential truth. What many refuse to realize is that you are true Israelites by blood and hold a special place in the heart of God The Most High! It was no coincidence that He chose Abraham to become the father of many nations. Abraham knew that there had to be a God much more powerful than the little idols that his father made for a profit, just like today's mega church preachers selling feel-good religion and prosperity for a profit, and just like the Catholic church, denounced by Martin Luther for selling indulgences—all prostituting the word of God. Abraham refused to worship the idols his father was selling, and he walked and trampled upon them before they were sold to people who held them sacred and worshipped them. Those people did not know that Lucifer is behind every single instance of idol worship, which gives him the energy to create more disasters upon mankind.

They forgot that all praise and worship belongs to God and God Alone. It's Lucifer who gets the praise whenever a person bows down to an idol or to any of God's creation, like the sun and moon and stars. Lucifer cannot break the eternal code and show himself, because he is forbidden to do so. But Satan doesn't care as long as people turn their praise from the true and living God and give it to something else—to the sun, the moon, the stars, or any idol made by the hands of man. Satan only cares that they are not giving their praise to The Creator, The Ancient of Days, but rather to him. Satan craves worship because he wants to be like God.

The Lord God of The Most High chose Abraham from all the other men on earth to manifest Himself through him, and Abraham, our father, did listen and glorify The Most High because he knew deep within his heart that there is something much bigger than the sun, moon, and stars of the sky that can be seen by mortal men. He realized that there is something even much bigger than what he could see with his naked eyes. He knew the story of Noah, though it has been swept under the rug because people seem to forget the things that matter most and cling to the things contrary to the love of God. Abraham knew that there was someone somewhere out there that holds the answer to the mystery of life and, like many of us, seeks to find the truth. And then the Lord came and made Himself known to Abraham, just like many today would like to know who they really are. I myself was once there, knowing that what I was feeling in my heart as a little boy was more than what people were telling me in church—that we are gentiles grafted into the family of God. I couldn't tell them what I was feeling inside because they would not understand. Picture a child who has loving parents yet still feels that something is missing, something that the child cannot put his finger on. Have you ever felt this way? That's how I felt as a little boy when I was told in church that I'm grafted into the family of God, through Jesus Christ. But what these preachers and teachers did not know is that Christ had been my trusted friend ever since I can remember, and He would speak to me as a Father speaks to his child. It was much deeper than just feeling like a step-child, a mysterious connection that I cannot explain. He was my best friend, though I kept that a secret for years. I would go and visit with Him in the woods and talk to Him there, with only my two dogs to hear our conversations, and they certainly didn't think I was crazy.

But if I said these things to anyone else they would laugh at me, and so my relationship with the Lord has been my little secret for all my life. When you know what you feel in your heart about the Lord God of The Most High, you need no one to tell you who you are. Every one of us is given the gift of being able to communicate with The One who has always loved you more than you'll ever know. I was sent to show the world's minorities that you must never believe what anyone thinks of you. What matters most is the relationship between you and The Lord God of The Most High, who made the ultimate sacrifice for us. Many of you are true blooded Israelites that have been scattered all over the world, as I have myself ended up in Jamaica, on a little hill called Glendevon in the town of Montego Bay. Who would have believed it if I had told them that I am a Levite? They would have laughed at me, because of the brainwashing that we have had to endure throughout our history of subjugation and persecution. But my life is not the result of random coincidence. It has been perfectly orchestrated. All the pitfalls, valleys, and mountains that have beset my path are a blessing in disguise, and who could have done this for me other than my heavenly Father. The secret behind the secret is that most of Israel was still in slavery for centuries, in the Americas and the rest of the world, including the West Indies, on a large scale. Do you think it was a mistake that we were scattered again after the great Exodus from Egypt and were then conquered by the Babylonians, as if we were lost forever. This is one of the greatest mysteries within the mystery of the secret plan of salvation—why Yashua The Christ, God's only Begotten, had to come, and not one of his angels. We are still scattered all over the world today, not understanding that one of the secrets behind the secret of Christ's second biggest reason for coming to earth was for the lost sheep of Israel, as it is written: "I was sent ONLY for the lost sheep of the house of Israel." And it is us who were scattered by Divine design to set the world on fire as children of The Most High God. Let no man fool you. It's time you understand who you really are. It is us who have to come back among the heathens and reestablish the fourth commandment among those who will be saved, because even William Miller and all the great reformers kept Sunday as the day of worship, though they were the pioneers in the battle against the dragon who has deceived the world and the very elect, if it was possible.

All those chosen by the Lord as his prophets and messengers to go and finish the work have got but a little piece of this great puzzle, which will forever be a mystery within a mystery, even after hundreds of thousands of years in heaven and in the world made new, those that will be saved will still be learning of this great mystery of The Most High God. Despite what He had given to Daniel and John the revelator and to prophets like Ezekiel and Isaiah, who had spoken of the coming of the messiah. Why was there only three wise men understood the significance of the star in the sky and the time of the birth of the King of Kings and came to worship Him?. This is the million dollar question you must never take for granted. God spoke to Hosea to show us how He speaks to the prophets: "And I gave numerous visions and through the prophets I gave parables" (Hosea 12:10). And today, many Jewish scholars have no clue of this great deceptive moment in time, as Christ said: "Many of them who have called themselves Jews are not Jews but are of the synagogue of Satan." Still waiting for the first coming of the messiah, they will be deceived into embracing the antichrist as messiah. What a great and sad day it will be. But it will happen. Every word that proceeded out of the mouth of God will come to fruition. They must, God help us! The gospel in the great commission was not meant to be preached so that everyone can be saved, because The All Wise God of the universe knows that this would not be possible. But it must be preached "AS A WITNESS TO ALL," and then shall come the END. Don't be deceived my friends. Don't wait for this great deception to pull us into the abyss of no return, in which even the very elect of God could be lost The secret behind the secret is that this great and troublesome deception will be entangled in these few words of Jesus Christ The Lord God of The Most High: "But for the elect's sake I'll cut the time short." The time will be shortened for those who are faithful unto the end.

Chapter 35

Don't Ever Give Up The Fight…

DON'T EVER GIVE UP THE FIGHT

Would Husain Bolt, the world's fastest runner ever (from the little island of Jamaica, I might add) ever stop running before reaching the finish line because he is out-running everyone else then claim he deserves a gold medal for winning the race? Think of this simple analogy before you ever stop running because you might feel tired. This is not the time to get tired. Slow down the pace if you must, but don't you ever give up or you and I will lose out on our eternal inheritance, which Satan intends to take from us in any way possible. You cannot let him deceive you, come what may. Remember, only those who are faithful unto the end of the journey shall be saved. Every man on the face of the earth has heard about Jesus Christ, in some way or another. It is now at the appointed time of "Whosoever will, may come." In 2 Timothy 4:1 – 8 it is written: "I charge thee therefore before God, and the Lord Jesus Christ, who shall judge the quick and the dead at his appearing and his kingdom; Preach the word; be instant in season, out of season; reprove, rebuke, exhort with all long suffering and doctrine. For the time will come when they will not endure sound doctrine; but after their own lusts shall they heap to themselves teachers, having itching ears; And they shall turn away their ears from the truth, and shall be turned unto fables. But watch thou in all things, endure afflictions, do the work of an evangelist, make full proof of thy ministry. For I am now ready to be offered, and the time of my departure is at hand. I have fought a good fight, I have finished my course, I have kept the faith: Henceforth there is laid up for me a crown of righteousness, which the Lord, the righteous judge, shall give me at that day: and not to me only, but unto all them also that love his appearing." We must have no love for this present world or for the wealth or education we enjoy or our position on earth—all the things we dread letting go of. Remember, it's never about the actuality of one's journey but rather the intent of the heart that the Lord looks upon. The beginning of the end is now the present we are living in. Don't ever wait until you think you've seen every prophecy fulfilled, because you can never see all that is taking place everywhere on the face of the earth. This great puzzle is so much bigger than we are. It is a mystery within a mystery that mortal mind will never be able to comprehend. It is up to you and me to make our calling sure as we learn to illuminate the corner where we are. As The Lord said, "just like in the days of Noah; so shall it be in the end." There were many in Noah's time who, with good intention, thought they could outwait The Lord, right up to the minute that the unseen hand closed the door forever. Don't let Satan, the old wicked and cunning devil serpent, con you out of your eternal rights. The fact is that the ultimate sacrifice has already granted us this heavenly privilege.

Don't ever give him the chance to deceive us a second time after all the warnings from The Lord God of The Most High Himself. He took the entire antediluvian world with him except for eight souls—Noah, his wife, their three sons, and their sons' wives. He then took everyone in Sodom and Gomorra with him except for four souls, and only three really escaped the destruction because Lot's wife's heart was still behind, and she looked back. To be with The Lord, you must be totally with Him because he will never accept forced love. Love given under duress is totally against His Holy eternal realm in which freedom of choice is paramount.

Chapter 36

We Cannot Serve God Out of Fear …It Has To Be Out of Love …Only

Can't you see the trend of the great deception? You think Satan won't do it again if he gets the chance? We cannot serve God based on feelings, or fear of burning in hell, but only out of love and by faith without borders. In this time you must live each moment in total consciousness, keenly aware of all of Satan's tricks and understanding that every moment from this day onward is a test— our last and final exam in this conscious state of mind. If we pass the test, we get to graduate from the University of Life, the college of mysticism and spirituality, and from wickedness in high and low places. Only the fittest of the fittest can ever survives. Those who will overcome such spiritual atrocity are the wise ones. These are men and women who learn the pitfalls and snares of the devil, who plays upon the conscience of men, disguised by the concealing cloak of creeping compromise that, if it were possible, would make even the very elect of God lose their way. Think again! You will be looking for a black cloak, but it will be nothing you'll ever expect it to be. We cannot out-smart Lucifer the Devil who have deceived billions and billions of God's holy angels, only Christ will be able to pull us through.

These are the slippery slopes to the mountain of God. Don't ever think it's going to be easy to understand the final laps in the race of life, as the rules are constantly changing. You will have to be more alert than ever before. Satan's intention is to divert you from the principles of God through creeping compromise. That's all it takes in the great deception for us to be lost. Our ticket to eternal life will have a steep price tag, but it has already been paid for upon the old rugged cross. All we have to do is claim it. We cannot do that through works alone, as you have seen, or by faith alone. If we learn how to combine both on the principles of love, as The Lord has warned us about, and learn to walk in His shadow as "The only Way, the truth, and the Life" amidst the trials and temptations to come, then you and I will be ready as the time draws near for the greatest graduation imaginable. The goal is not to graduate, like you're in high school and wanted that high GPA (grade point average)grade to be able to go the college or university of your dream like to the schools of the prospective- president like Yale and Harvard and the rest of the ivy-league institutions of America and the rest of the world.

This will without a doubt be the test of time , it's not to be overly ambitious or confident, but rather with humility of heart, trusting The Lord to see us through, even with a barely passing grade. That's not going to be easy. I warn you again with these simple but prophetic words, "ITS NOT GOING TO BE EASY." If you and I are going to be victorious, it will only be by remaining faithful unto the end. If you and I should exit now, it would be an eternal loss, but if we keep our eyes on the prize we will be able to fly away from this wickedly sad, sinful and dreadful world ,with the Lord God when He returns to claim His own.

Learn the parables of Jesus Christ with the sermons on the mount, because in them lies the key to mystery within a mystery, and they may hold the very answers to the kingdom of heaven. Learn to put your trust only in The Lord God of The Most High, who is the only way to "THE ANCIENT Of DAYS," and Him only we must serve. A word to the wise is sufficient. The tribulation president is here.

Don't wait until it's too late like the antediluvians did, hoping that the words of Noah would go away. Hoping that he was a drunk ,and doesn't know what he is talking about. What is to come is like nothing we've seen before just like they have never seen the rain, once it start falling it was no more a place to contemplate all that you have heard.

Hoping that you will sum up the courage and make a decision for tomorrow. But this time there was no more a place to go and think about all of what Noah had told them. Are we entering that very moment in time when all of the above that I have talked about the best way I can ,not as a writer, but someone who was given a message to give to you. Will it be in vain?

I know it's hard to believe some of the things I've told you...I myself was amazed that He would have come to someone like me, a man who is perfectly flawed and is so underserving of His mercy much less His love. He could have chosen one of the famous and popular preachers men like Billy Graham or T D Jakes, and all the well know preachers of the day ,who have oratorical skill to convey such timely and sensitive matters that the world need to know about, and then decides for themselves. But somehow it doesn't seems that way, because they would have let the world know what was shown to them. But it is not wise for men to fabricate things of God stating that The Lord God speak to them in dreams and visions, when He haven't, much less to hear his voice calling you from the heavens of heavens in this time, when they say He haven spoken to man face to face in thousands of years. For some reason my journey is a little different as these experiences humbles me and draw me closer to Him.

I was taken up into His holy mountain and saw things that still blows my mind , looking at The Great ONE who have given the ten commandment to Moses. And have chosen Abraham to be the one to carry the torch of the essential truth in a dark world. To remind humankind of His ways and principles that would be fulfilled in his children who God promise to make them like the sand of the sea and as plentiful as the stars above.

He would later speak to Abraham about destroying Sodom and Gomorrah, as an example of what the world will look like when He return to earth for the great and wicked day that Lucifer feared the most, never knowing that it would really come this soon. After thousands and thousands of years that was allotted to him to do what he does best , which is to create havoc and suffering and pain to Gods children, well that time is now coming to an end ,like everything that has a beginning has an ending. This is the beginning of the end that no mortal man knows how long it will last, this is one of the mystery within a mystery that no man knows or have the answer to.

The Lord is not slack in His promises. He means what He says, and says what He means. It is us as fallible men that is unwise and think that we know the mysteries of God .

He is the same One that have invited me up into His holy mountain and then sent for me to come and meet with Him in heaven and what I saw , I did not know that He The Lord God of The Most High would show it to mortal men. Much less me a man who is perfectly flawed.

I invite you to come with me as we journey through the black books of Moses its secrets and last prophecies, let's see what next we'll find in the rise of the tribulation president. Things that will come on his plate to partake of that he doesn't have a clue will come his way. He will have to choose when America reaches the cross road of no return. The cross road of the great divide is on our doorstep.

Remember this little parable when you're in the jungle and run into a hungry tiger what will he do? It will wait for the right moment to devoure you even if you climb a tree you will become its meal unless somebody rescues you. The truth of the matter is that you will not be able to out-smart it, the moment you think it has walked away and you decide to come down from that tree and run for it, is the very moment you're going to run right into its deadly unforgiving eyes , not realizing that it's been watching your every move if it didn't come up into the tree and eat you alive.

The only escape is to get out of the jungle while you can. Don't wait until you spot the tiger, because once you see it, it already saw you long before you realized. Also please don't wait until the storm is at your doorstep. before you start packing your bag to run. Learn from the past. These are warnings that you must not take for granted.

I beg you to heed these forecasts that were given to me to give to you. I try not to call them prophetic forecast, not wanting to put self into the picture, calling myself any kind of prophet because God knows that's not my intention. My mission or assignment is to make you be aware of the deadly and great deception that is here and you can't see it hovering over our heads. This might be the final warning because before you know it might be too late. I'll show you more of what The Lord has shown me it will be up to you to take heed............ I can only show you the rest will be up to you.

Everything is going to happen overnight, as I have stated at the beginning of this narrative pray that today is not too late, and we don't put this off for tomorrow, because tomorrow is the easy escape from the reality that is in front of us.

Not realizing that it's really an idea that is not promise to any of us. The dormancy of hate still lingers in the heart of many of our

The Rise of the Tribulation President
225

countrymen.

It will only be a matter of time before they rise up and reclaim what they think is rightfully theirs.

There will be a worldwide economic collapse, this melt-down will be by design, but will take everyone by surprise as its effect overspill into the rest of the world, and become real.

This president will play on the emotion of his most loyal followers who will see nothing wrong with his rhetoric, or vice-versa of segregation and anti-Semitism shouting from the mouth of his most loyal supporters, where blacks, Jews and Muslims, children of the minority race will be in for a rude awakening when they think that they will be welcome at the table of making America great again….

The fear of poverty and mediocrity wrapped up with the unsurety of hate or dislike will echo high above the news pundit or so-call fake news carriers (as they are called) as they themselves will join this revolution of making America great again, as time dwindles down into a different reality.

Bitter fights will break out in the streets of America, much bigger than what they are now and without a doubt will sway public opinion as confusion paralyze our moral compass. Even though some whites will hate the idea of this great segregation that will return after a while most will find themselves, drawn to a common idea even though they might not totally agree.

Many believe that this president will be their savior bringing back the old days, but sad to say we've all been deceived. What is to come is much bigger than the president himself, he is put in power to implement laws that is already on the books and also using the executive order to make heads spin, especially those who do not believe. He will use threats after threats to soften his opponents, the congress or the senate who comes up against him

There will be much marching in the streets of America as rising tension will give president to the seizure of property and arrest made.

There will be repeating of history taking place right on our door steps and there will not be any sympathizers this time because everyman will be looking out for himself. The world will see once more what human being are capable of doing to each other ,this time it will be nothing we've seen before. If you don't know what to look for you'll never escape what is about to come upon us. I'll show you more of some of what was made privy to me; knowledge is power, fools do not take instructions. In my last dream all I saw were truck loads, upon truckloads of soldiers positioning themselves for the final moment in TIME.

Again I cannot tell myself what to see or what is privy to me in dreams and visions, I'm telling you this because of the things that I'm seeing are now coming true faster than I have expected.

Many of the religious people especially the evangelical Christians in America who believe that president Trump will be the savior, over-turning the policies of president Obama with his liberal ideals with homosexuality the law of the land with same sex marriage will be one of the most deceptive pill that they'll ever swallow.

Sad to say that because of these policies they think was trust upon them , they will turn blind eye to the atrocity that is about to come upon mankind and upon us as a nation. Some of them in their hearts really thinking that they're doing the right thing, but will realize when it's too late that they have been deceived. Many will find themselves on the wrong side of God's plan if they don't wake up before it's too late.

I must warn you, president Trump is a prophetic president, which have nothing to do with you and I putting him into power. Whoever ran against him would have lost just the same as Mrs. Clinton. I will show you some of the things that was shown to me a man born and bred in poverty and is still perfectly flawed yet The Lord choses to show me these things.

It is now Gods TIME, man's time has already run out and soon our moment in time will be expired sooner than we will ever believe it. What is to be will be, and you will realize that nothing we do or say will be able to stop what is already here.

May God help us!! and may we ask for wisdom and with it understanding to help us through these sad and gloomy days that lie ahead. The Good Lord be with you Always

- Mutti Lewis

(Blessed love)

Chapter 37

Will Christ be… The Last Alternative?

Will the Lord God of The Most high be our last choice in life ? When we have done everything, and some …..how fair will it be to try and use God as the last alternative? Will we be able to get away with it in these tribulation times? Let see. For several months in 2015 there was speculation about the possibility of President Obama being elected to a third term. Not only is this impossible without a constitutional amendment, which would take years to pass, but it also went against the political and prophetic forecast that I was privy to. The secret behind the secret is that the tribulation president could not be a man with empathy or deep feelings for his fellow citizens. It had to be a hardliner, and that's exactly what we got in Donald Trump. The seven years of tribulation will come as creeping compromise. It is time for us to find ourselves and decide where we will spend eternity. The biggest question is, "Will your zip code be in the kingdom of heaven or will it be in hell?" There is no middle ground.

I predicted way ahead of the pundits that Trump would win the Republican nomination. It was only Joe Scarborough and Mika Levinsky on MSNBC's Morning Joe program that saw what I had seen long before the final countdown. Welcome to the beginning of the great tribulation starting in 2017. This will end in 2024, as America will re-elect Trump to finish the job of making America great again. God help those who live to tell their story, because everything is going to be unlike anything you have ever seen before. Everything that is to come will happen rapidly. You will not have time to think, and before you know it, it will all be over. It's going to be sad for many of us that time is going to creep up on us and leave without saying goodbye. The Antichrist will usher in the new world order in its full power, and the National Sunday Law will be implemented in its full force. By this time everyone will have their mark or their chip to be able to buy and sell or run and hide. There will be no middle ground: the mark of the beast or the seal of Jesus Christ. You choose. You will realize that the fourth commandment is and will be the problem.

It might sound a bit farfetched but you will be surprise what you're going to wake up to one of these morning. You're going to see things in the heavens that are not of humankind and you're going to want to cry and the tears will not come, you'll want to run and realize that there's no place to run. It will be the day you wish you were never born.

You'll realize that only a personal relationship with The Most High God that will be able to deliver you from all of the above. It cannot be by fear, or been scared of going to hell, none of this will help you, but I can show you how.

This again, I must emphasize with clarity; It's not going to be any kind of scare tactics to the kingdom of heaven . The fear of death and hell will not take you there or save you from what is to come. The secret behind the secret is that the key to the kingdom of heaven is hidden in the mystery of the parables.

Only those who seek diligently with their hearts will find it .Only those who knock from the depts of their hearts the door will be open to, the secret is that it has to be before the rain starts falling.

If you had it in mind to knock, you better start knocking now; if you have it in mind to ask you better start asking those question now, because once the rain starts drizzling its already too late I can only show you how to escape what is to come. Blessed Love to All

Mutti Lewis

Yashua The Christ should not be the last alternative in our lives, if so be the case it will be too late by the time you think and realize that the world has really come to an end.

You must understand that the moment in TIME is NOW don't continue to believe it's around the corner, and you still have time to make up your mind. These very words will come to haunt you as you watch it come to fruition . "Ye that is filthy let him be filthy still…..he that is just let him be just still …..ye that is holy let him be holy still….ye that is righteous , let him be righteous still" Revelation 22:11

You'll find the answer in the next chronicles. But first you must see how the tribulation president will play his hand and how it's going to affect every man who is alive and are living on earth…………. The Rise of The Tribulation President Vol. 2 …… 2nd Edition will give you the answers just as how The Lord God has shown it to me.

"I wish you all the best of luck and pray and hope that there is still TIME" God help us!!

(To be continued) In Vol. 2 ……..

www.ingramcontent.com/pod-product-compliance
Lightning Source LLC
Chambersburg PA
CBHW032223080426
42735CB00008B/684